HARCOURT HORIZONS

World Regions

Activity Book

Teacher's Edition

Harcourt

Orlando   Austin   Chicago   New York   Toronto   London   San Diego

Visit *The Learning Site!*
www.harcourtschool.com

The activities in this book reinforce social studies concepts and skills in *Harcourt Horizons: World Regions*. There is one activity for every lesson and skill in the Pupil Edition. Copies of the activity pages appear with answers in the Teacher's Edition. In addition to activities, this book also contains reproductions of the graphic organizers that appear in the chapter reviews in the Pupil Edition. Multiple-choice test preparation pages for student practice are also provided. A blank multiple-choice answer sheet can be found after these table of contents pages.

Contents

Introduction

·UNIT·

1

Chapter 1

Chapter 2

Name ____ Date _________________________

Multiple-Choice
Answer Sheet

**Number your answers to match the questions
on the test preparation page.**

MAP AND GLOBE SKILLS
Read a Map

Directions Maps are drawings that show places on Earth. A map can help you find the locations of countries, cities, landforms, and bodies of water. Maps have many special features that help you read the information they contain. Study the list of map features below. Some of the features have been correctly identified on the map. Fill in the missing names of features in the spaces below.

compass rose   inset map   map key   map title

grid   locator   map scale

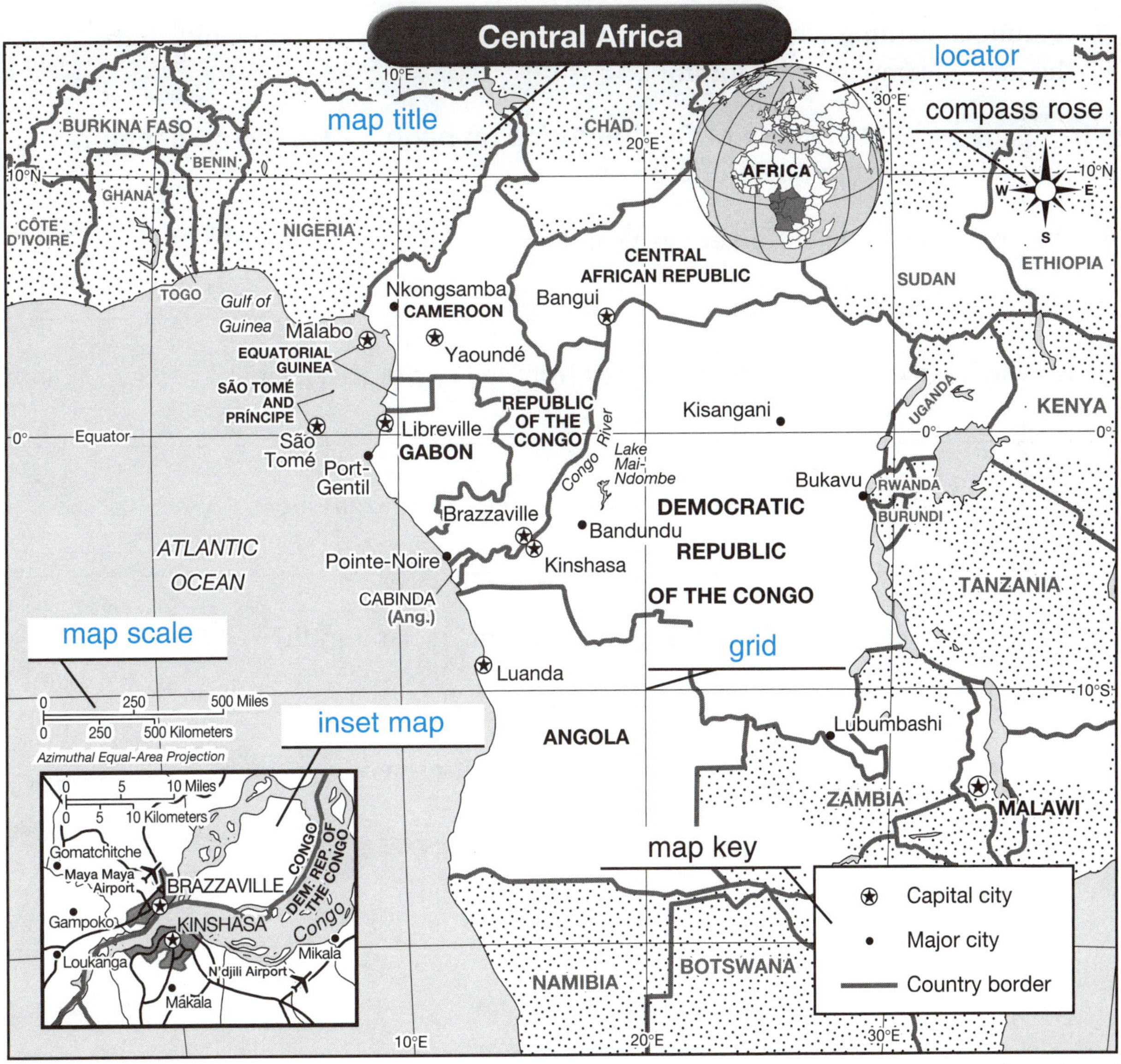

(continued)

Name ____   Date ___________________________

 Study the map of Central Africa on page 1. Then read each of
the situations below. Underline the name of the correct map feature that
helps to solve the problem.

1 A travel agent searching for a map of Central Africa would read the
(map keys / <u>map titles</u>) to find the correct one.

2 A student would use a (<u>compass rose</u> / map key) to learn the direction of
Equatorial Guinea from Luanda, Angola.

3 A cartographer would use a (map key / <u>map scale</u>) to figure out the distance
between Kinshasa and Libreville.

4 A tourist who wants to find the location of the Kinshasa airport would use the
(<u>inset map</u> / locator).

5 A student learning where Central Africa is located in the world would study
the map's (compass rose / <u>locator</u>).

 Study the map of Central Africa on page 1. Use the map features
to help you answer the questions below.

6 Which countries share Cameroon's southern border? Equatorial Guinea, Gabon,
and the Republic of the Congo

7 In which direction is São Tomé located from the city of Kisangani?
west

8 Is Yaoundé or Bangui farther away from the city of Brazzaville?
Bangui

9 Which is a capital city—Libreville, Lubumbashi, or Bandundu?
Libreville

10 Is the city of Makala a suburb of Brazzaville or Kinshasa? Kinshasa

                          Use after reading Skill Lesson, pages A2–A3.

Why Geography Matters

Directions Geographers study Earth in different ways. Some geographers use five topics called the five themes of geography. Others use six topics called the six essential elements of geography. Review the pictures below. Then choose the theme or essential element that a geographer would think about if he or she was studying the information in the picture. Some questions may have more than one correct answer. Write the letters of the best answers on the lines next to the pictures.

1 _____ C _____ 

A. Location
B. Places and Regions
C. Movement

2 _____ A, C _____ 

A. Environment and Society
B. The World in Spatial Terms
C. Human-Environment Interactions

3 _____ B _____ 

A. Places and Regions
B. The World in Spatial Terms
C. Location

4 _____ C _____ 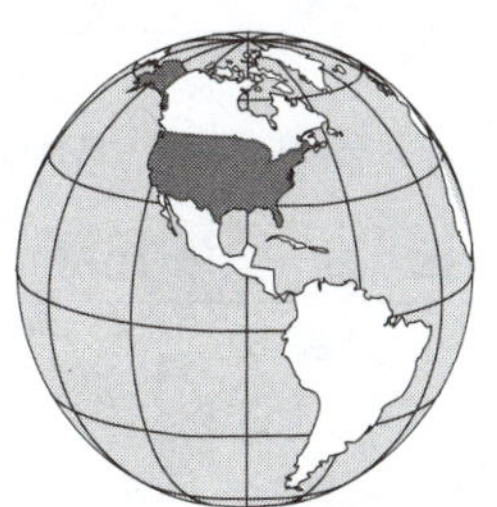

A. Place
B. Physical Systems
C. Location

5 _____ C _____ 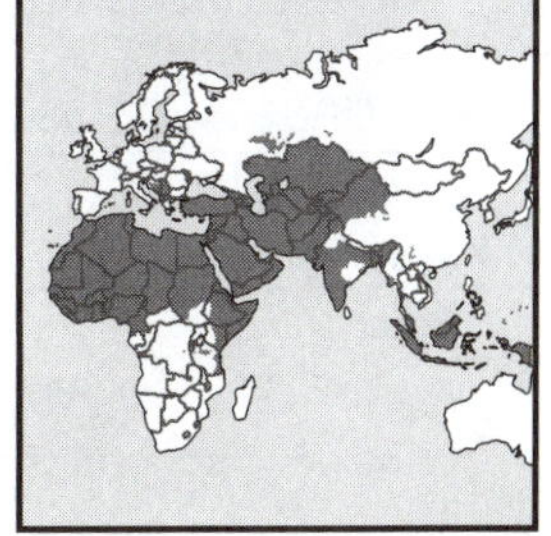

A. Physical Systems
B. The Uses of Geography
C. Places and Regions

Why History Matters

Directions Historians look for
clues about the past when they study
objects that people have left behind.
Objects teach us about people's
clothes, food, trade, and other parts
of their daily lives. Imagine you are
a historian who has just found an old
Viking settlement. Your team has
uncovered many objects. Study the
objects and use them to answer
the questions that follow.

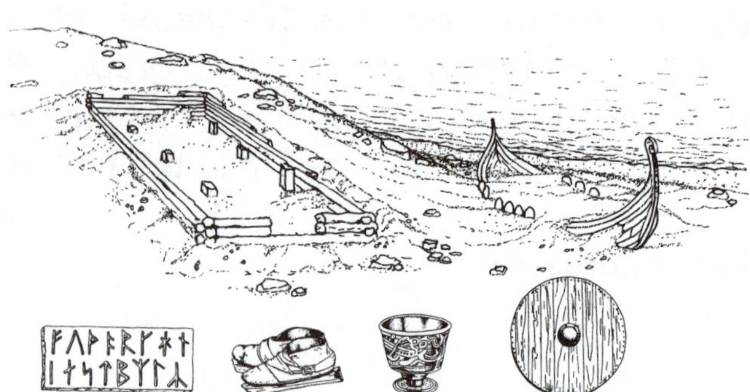

1 What do the ice skates teach us
about the daily lives of the Viking
people?

Possible response: The ice skates show that Vikings used ice skates for

transportation or recreation. They also show that the Vikings used available

materials to make objects.

2 What do the shield and longship teach us about the Vikings?

Possible response: These objects suggest that the Vikings were a war-like people

who needed these objects for battle.

3 Why is the silver cup from Britain an important find? Possible response: The silver

cup from Britain suggests that the Vikings had contact with the British people.

4 What does the alphabet teach us about the Viking culture?

Possible response: The alphabet shows that the Viking people had a written form

of their language.

READING SKILLS

Compare Primary and Secondary Sources

Directions Primary sources are firsthand accounts of historical events. Secondary sources are descriptions of events written later. Below are two accounts of the Japanese surrender that ended World War II. Read each source and compare them by answering the questions that follow.

From a radio message dated August 14, 1945, by Emperor Hirohito

After pondering deeply the general trends of the world and the actual conditions obtaining in Our Empire today, We have decided to effect a settlement of the present situation by resorting to an extraordinary measure. The war situation has developed not necessarily to Japan's advantage. Moreover, the enemy has begun to employ a new and most cruel bomb. Should We continue to fight, it would not only result in an ultimate collapse and obliteration of the Japanese nation, but also it would lead to the total extinction of human civilization. This is the reason why We have ordered the acceptance of the provisions of the Joint Declaration of the Powers.

A Country Study from the Library of Congress

After initial naval and battlefield successes and a tremendous over extension of its resources in the war . . . Japan was unable to sustain "Greater East Asia" [the Japanese Empire]. After the detonation of atomic bombs over Hiroshima and Nagasaki on August 6 and 8, 1945, the emperor asked that the Japanese people bring peace to Japan . . . by surrendering to the Allied powers. The documents of surrender were signed on board the U.S.S. Missouri in Tokyo Bay on September 2, 1945. The terms of surrender included the occupation of Japan by Allied military forces . . . and surrender of Japan's colonial holdings.

1 Which source is the primary source? Explain how you know.

The radio message from Emperor Hirohito is the primary source because it gives his actual words at the time he surrendered.

2 Which of the sources gives more detail about the actual surrender of Japan?

The Library of Congress's Country Study provides more details.

3 Does the primary or secondary source have examples of bias within it? Explain your answer. The primary source has examples of the Emperor Hirohito's bias, including his belief that the United States would destroy human civilization.

Why Culture and Society Matters/
Why Civics and Government Matters/
Why Economics Matters

Directions The statements below describe countries or regions you will learn about in your textbook. Decide if each of the statements refers to the culture, society, civic rights and responsibilities, government, or economy of the country or region. Write the vocabulary term that best describes the statement. Use your textbook to help you review the vocabulary before you begin.

Vocabulary
Civic rights and responsibilities
Culture
Economy
Government
Society

1 Today many South American countries have a middle class made up mostly of business workers and professional people. Most South Americans, however, belong to the lower classes.

Society ____

2 Brunei is a kind of monarchy called a sultanate. A leader called

a sultan rules it. The sultan has a cabinet. Government _________

3 For many years, Mexicans worked in primary industries—farming and mining. In the 1940s, many Mexicans started working in manufacturing. Mexicans now manufacture many of the finished products

they buy and use. Economy _____________________________

4 Australians speak English, but in their own special ways. They also adopted

Aborigine words such as *jumbuck*, which means "sheep." Culture ______

5 Australians and New Zealanders are aware of the importance of conserving their environments and wildlife. Environmentalists have influenced governments to

protect the land and wildlife. Civic rights and responsibilities ______

6 In China people are not allowed to say anything bad about the government. Newspapers and television stations are censored. This means they cannot print or

broadcast anything the government does not allow. government ________

7 In African villages, elders met to discuss problems and agree on solutions. Even in many cultures where a king led the people, a council of advisers made the most

important decisions. Government ________________________

Earth's Landforms

Directions Earth's surface changes in many ways. Weathering, erosion, and deposition affect Earth's shape. Human activities such as building structures and farming also change Earth. Review each of the definitions and study the landscape below. Then circle and label all the examples of weathering, erosion, deposition, and human activities that you can find in the landscape.

Weathering: The process of breaking up rocks into smaller pieces, or sediment, by water, glaciers, and wind

Erosion: The process of moving sediment

Deposition: The process of dropping sediment in a new location

Human Activities: Changes people make

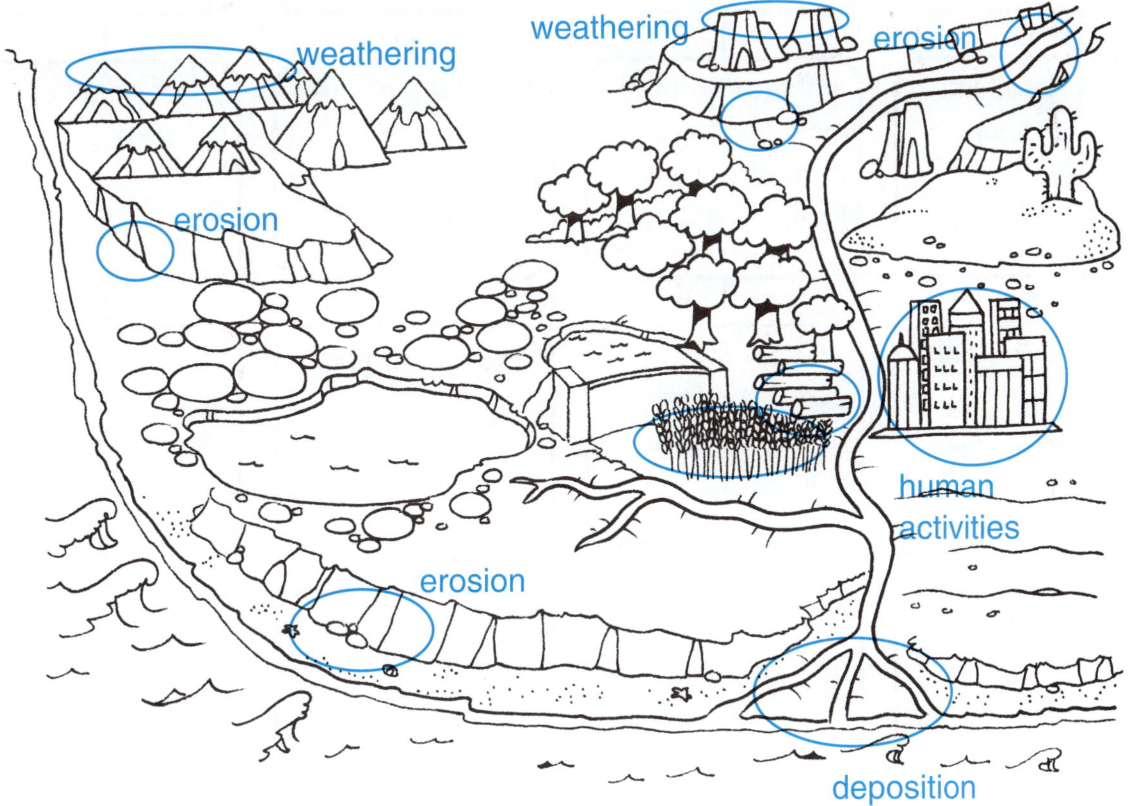

Directions Read the question. Write your answer on the lines provided.

How have human activities changed this landscape?

Humans have changed the land by building a large city on land that was once part of a plain and a forest. The humans have also cleared the land to plant their crops.

Earth's Bodies of Water

Directions Earth has many different kinds of bodies of water. Read their names in the graphic organizer below. Then fill in the columns with statements that describe how bodies of water are formed and details that make each kind different from the others.

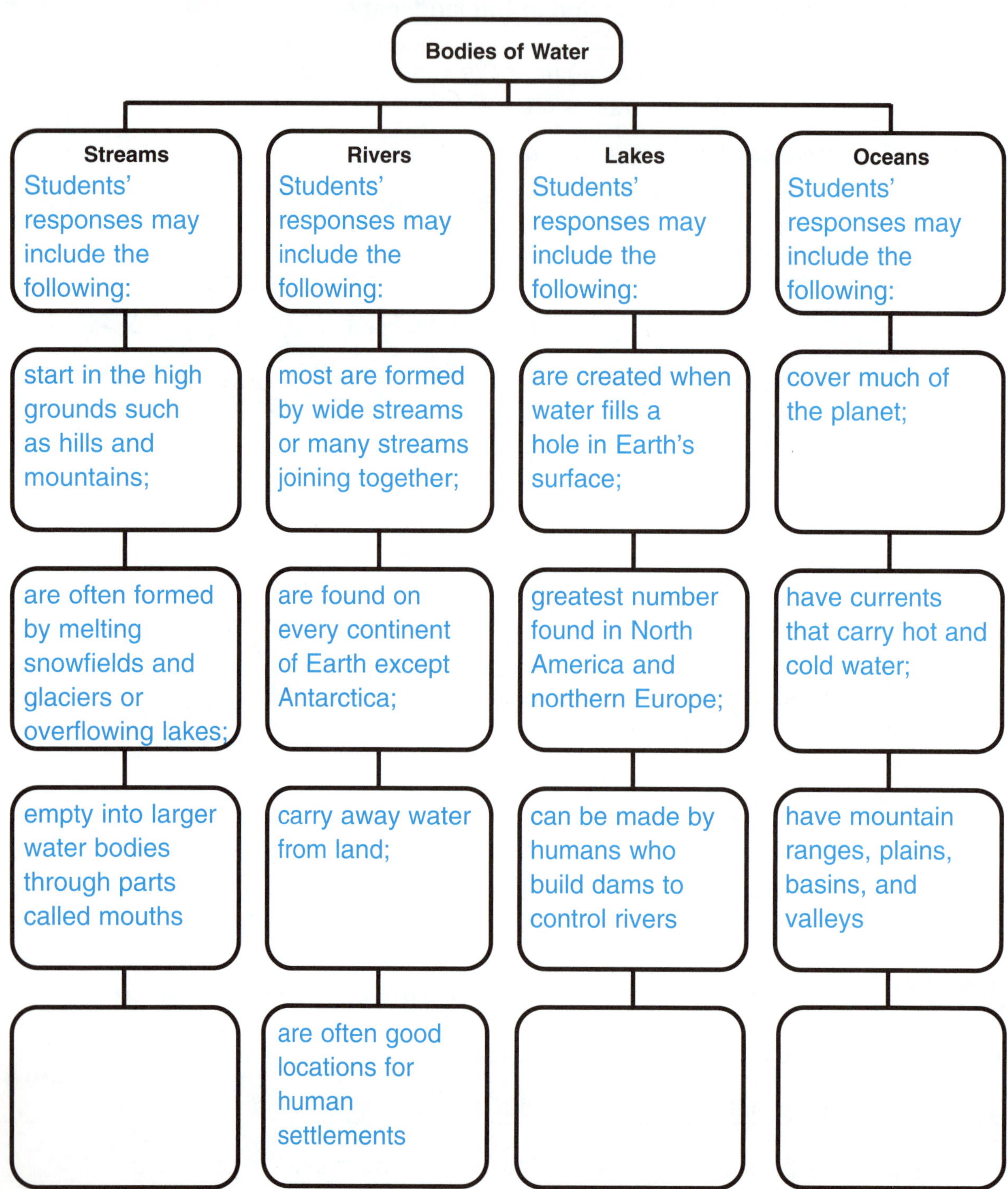

   Use after reading Chapter 1, Lesson 2, pages 26–31.

MAP AND GLOBE SKILLS

Use Latitude and Longitude

Directions   Study the map. Look closely at the lines of latitude and the lines of longitude. Then use the map to help you answer the questions that follow.

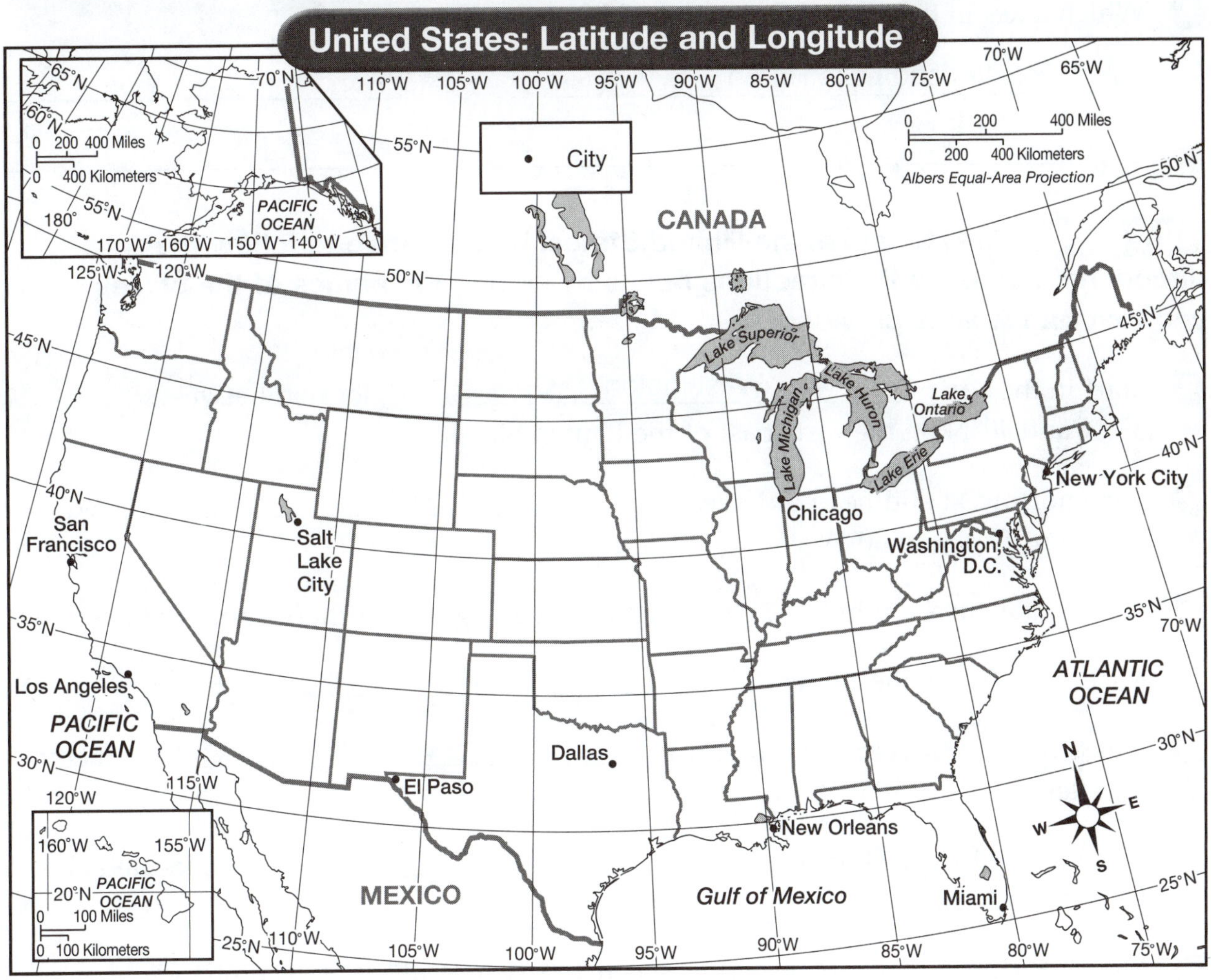

United States: Latitude and Longitude

1 Which city is located between 115°W and 120°W?

Los Angeles

2 Which city is located where 30°N and 90°W cross?

New Orleans

(continued)

3 Which city on the map is the closest to 40°N and 75°W?

New York City ____

4 Which bodies of water does 25°N cross?

The Pacific Ocean, the Gulf of Mexico, and the Atlantic Ocean ________________

5 Which lakes in the United States does 45°N pass through?

Lake Michigan and Lake Huron ____

____

Directions **Travel across the United States! Use the map to follow the directions. Complete the directions below by writing the names of the places you visit on the lines provided.**

6 Start in the city of _________ Washington, D.C. _________, located between 35°N and 40°N on the east coast of the United States.

7 Turn northwest and head to Lake ____________ Ontario ____________, located between 75°W and 80°W.

8 At the lake, turn southwest to the city located along the southern shore of Lake

Michigan. This is the city of ____________ Chicago ____________.

9 Now continue traveling southwest to ____________ El Paso ____________, a city that lies closest to 105°W.

10 Moving northwest, stop at ____________ Salt Lake ____________ City, located close to 40°N and 112°W.

11 Your last stop is in a city located between 120°W and 125°W. Welcome to

____________ San Francisco ____________.

Earth's Climates and Vegetation

Directions **Read the following paragraph and study the diagram to help you answer the questions below.**

Climate is the kind of weather a place has over long periods of time. Altitude has a major effect on mountain climates. Every 1,000 feet (305m) the land rises, the air turns colder by 3 degrees Fahrenheit (1.7 degrees Celsius). Altitude also affects the climate of a place through the weather. As air rises over one side of the mountain, it turns colder and loses moisture in the form of rain and snow. As the now dry air passes over to the other side of the mountain, it drops closer to the ground and begins warming. As the air warms, it absorbs moisture from the land around it. This side of the mountain is called the rain shadow. The area affected by the rain shadow has a much drier climate.

1 How are the climate and land on the left side of the mountain different from the climate and land on the right side? The climate on the left side of the mountain has more precipitation. The result is that the land receives water constantly and is lush and fertile. On the right side, the dry air absorbs water from the land. As a result, there is very little precipitation and the land is arid.

2 How might the rain shadow affect human activities? Student responses might include how the arid land in the rain shadow is not ideal for establishing cities or farmlands due to the lack of available water.

Natural Resources

Directions Underline the word or group of words in parentheses that best completes each sentence.

1 Graphite is a (<u>mineral resource</u>/biological resource) that is used to make pencils.

2 Fossil fuels are (renewable/<u>nonrenewable</u>) resources because they cannot be replaced within a reasonable time.

3 Using less water is one example of how people can (recycle/<u>conserve</u>) resources.

4 Some mineral resources called (chemicals/<u>fossil fuels</u>) are used to provide energy.

5 (<u>Trees</u>/Petroleum and gas) are resources that help clean the air and are a source of wood for homes and furniture.

Directions Match the energy descriptions on the left with the energy sources on the right.

Energy

6 __C__ Electricity created by air flowing over a special engine called a turbine.

7 __D__ This is energy created by the sun heating water and changing it into steam.

8 __A__ The fuel produced from this is used to power automobiles around the world.

9 __B__ Electricity made by water flowing over a turbine engine.

10 __E__ This mineral resource is burned to create heat energy that heats homes.

11 __F__ In many countries people burn this biological resource to heat their homes and cook their food.

Energy Sources

A. petroleum

B. tidal energy

C. wind power

D. solar power

E. coal

F. wood

CITIZENSHIP SKILLS
Solve a Problem

Directions Read about the problem of water pollution and the five steps to solve it. Put the statements in order by writing the letter of each one next to the correct step in the problem-solving process.

Fresh water is an important natural resource that is automatically renewed by the water cycle. Water pollution prevents the water cycle from resupplying Earth with fresh water. Much of the water pollution comes from our own homes. Motor oil from leaking automobiles is swept into the sewer systems and pollutes the water of streams, rivers, and lakes. Water pollution damages marine life and the health of people and animals who drink it.

Solving the Water Pollution Problem

A. It would also be better for the environment to fix the motor oil leak. Parking the automobile away from the sewers will not stop it from polluting the water.

B. How do we prevent motor oil from our automobile from being washed down our driveways and causing water pollution?

C. We cleaned the oil from the driveway, we fixed the automobile so that it no longer leaks motor oil. The driveway is clean, and no motor oil is leaking into the sewer system.

D. Bring the car to a mechanic to fix the oil leak.

E. We can fix the automobiles to stop them from leaking motor oil, or we can park our automobiles away from the sewer system.

Problem-Solving Process

1 __B__ Identify the problem.

2 __E__ Think of possible solutions.

3 __A__ Look at the facts of the situation and compare how each solution would work.

4 __D__ Plan a way to carry out the solution.

5 __C__ Evaluate the solution and think about how well it solves the problem.

The World's Geography

Directions Complete this graphic organizer to show that you understand how to identify the main idea and the supporting details for each lesson of Chapter 1.

MAIN IDEA → DETAILS

LESSON 1 MAIN IDEA:

Earth's landforms have been shaped and reshaped over time.

Detail: Students may mention tectonic plates, lava from volcanoes, and weathering by water, wind, and ice.

LESSON 2 MAIN IDEA:

Earth's bodies of water support life on the planet.

Detail: Students may mention that bodies of water provide transportation, as well as water for drinking, cleaning, and energy.

LESSON 3 MAIN IDEA:

Earth, the sun, the oceans, and the wind interact to produce Earth's varied climates.

Detail: Students may mention that a region's climate is affected by wind patterns, the angle of the sun's rays, and how close the region is to large bodies of water.

LESSON 4 MAIN IDEA:

Earth's natural resources are important to people.

Detail: Students may mention the role of trees in reducing pollution and producing oxygen, the role of fertile soil in producing food, the role of fossil fuels in providing energy.

Name _______________________ Date _______________

1 Test Preparation

Directions Read each question and choose the best answer. Then fill in the circle for the answer you have chosen. Be sure to fill in the circle completely.

1 What impact does a rain shadow have on the land below it?
- Ⓐ It causes Earth's tectonic plates to slide.
- Ⓑ It causes the air to rise over the land.
- Ⓒ It causes rain and snow to fall on the land.
- **Ⓓ** It causes the dry air to absorb moisture from the land.

2 The largest amount of fresh water can be found in—
- **Ⓕ** frozen glaciers and ice caps.
- Ⓖ water vapor in the air.
- Ⓗ dampness in the soil.
- Ⓙ lakes and rivers.

3 If it is summer in the Northern Hemisphere, then which statement is true?
- **Ⓐ** The Northern Hemisphere is tilted toward the sun.
- Ⓑ The Northern Hemisphere is entirely above the Tropic of Cancer.
- Ⓒ It is summer in the Southern Hemisphere, too.
- Ⓓ The sun's rays are vertical at 23.5 degrees south latitude.

4 A nonrenewable resource is—
- Ⓕ wind power.
- Ⓖ forests.
- Ⓗ water.
- **Ⓙ** oil and natural gas.

5 What effect do arid climates have on vegetation?
- Ⓐ Vegetation does not grow in arid climates.
- Ⓑ Vegetation grows in dense clusters.
- **Ⓒ** Vegetation grows far apart with long roots.
- Ⓓ Vegetation grows without roots.

Population and Settlement

Directions Read the paragraph and study the chart below, which shows four circle graphs. Then use the chart to answer the questions.

The movement of people on Earth is called migration. Some people migrate, or leave, their homeland for economic opportunities and better lives. These people are known by international law as **immigrants.** Others are forced from their home by war and unfair treatment. These people are known as **refugees.** According to the United Nations, there have been about 22.3 million refugees in recent years. In many countries they make up a large part of the population. The circle graphs below show the total population of four countries and the percent of people who have been pushed from these places during 1999–2000.

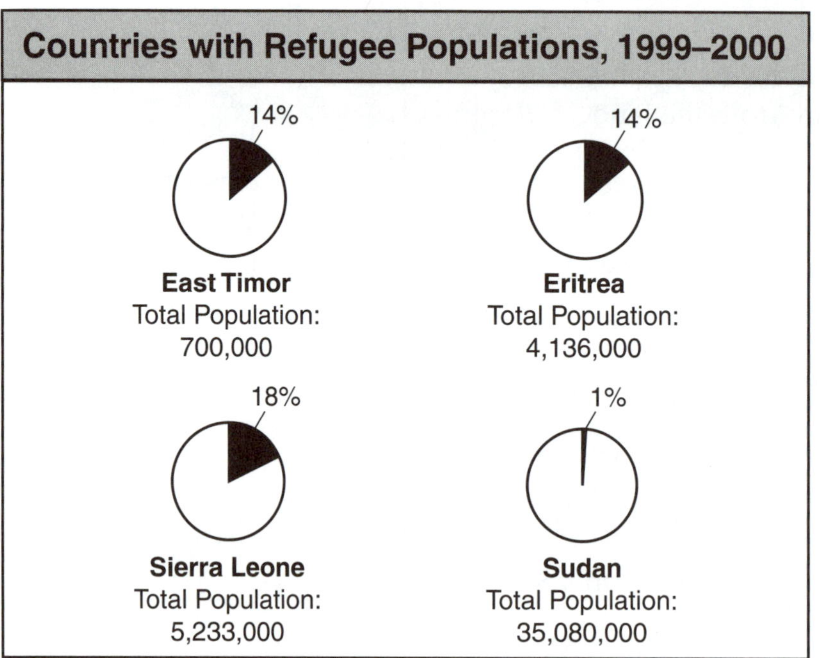

1 Which country had the largest percent of refugees? Which country had the smallest? Sierra Leone had the largest, and Sudan had the smallest.

2 Both Eritrea and East Timor lost 14 percent of their population. Which country had the greater number of citizens outside its borders? Eritrea

3 Look closely at the total population and the percent of refugees for these countries. Which country had the highest number of refugees? Sierra Leone, with about 942,000 people

MAP AND GLOBE SKILLS
Read a Population Map

Directions Study the map below. Pay close attention to the population density patterns of Asia. Use the map and an atlas to help you complete the map.

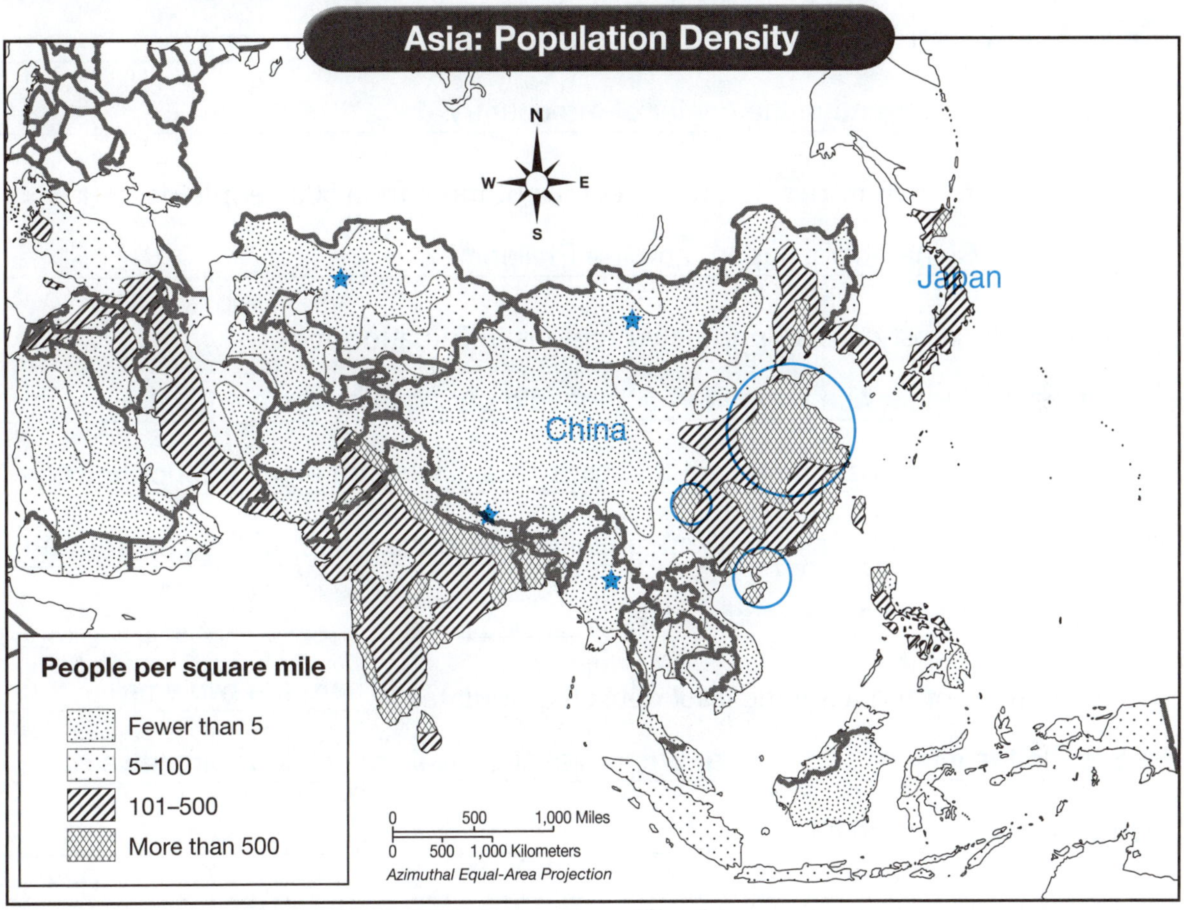

Asia: Population Density

1 On the map, label the East Asian country that has fewer than 5 people per square mile in its western regions and more than 500 people per square mile along its eastern coast.

2 On the map, label the East Asian island country that has a population density of mostly 101–500 people per square mile.

3 Draw stars on the four countries on the map that have fewer than five people per square mile in most areas.

4 Circle the areas of China that have more than 500 people per square mile.

(continued)

Directions **Use the map on the previous page as well as an atlas to help you answer the questions that follow.**

5 What is the population density for most of Saudi Arabia?

fewer than 5 people per square mile

6 Where are Saudi Arabia's densest regions located? The densest regions of Saudi Arabia, with 5 to 100 people per square mile, are located along the southwestern coast and in the center of the country.

7 What are the four countries that have regions of more than 500 people per square mile? China, India, Japan, and the Philippines

8 Where are the most densely populated regions in India located?

The regions of India with more than 500 people per square mile are located along India's southwestern and southeastern coastlines and along the northern border of the country. There is also a small region in the center of the country with more than 500 people per square mile.

9 Which regions of India are the least densely populated? There are two small regions in the interior of India that are the least densely populated, with fewer than five people per square mile.

10 Study both China and India on the map. Which country has larger regions with more than 500 people per square mile? China

11 How are the population density patterns of China and India similar? How are they different? Both have areas of high population density, both have high population densities near their coasts; almost all of India has a high population density while large parts of China have low population densities.

Cultures and Societies

Directions Complete the puzzle by filling in the correct term for each definition below. Then unscramble the circled letters to help you find the word that will complete the paragraph below.

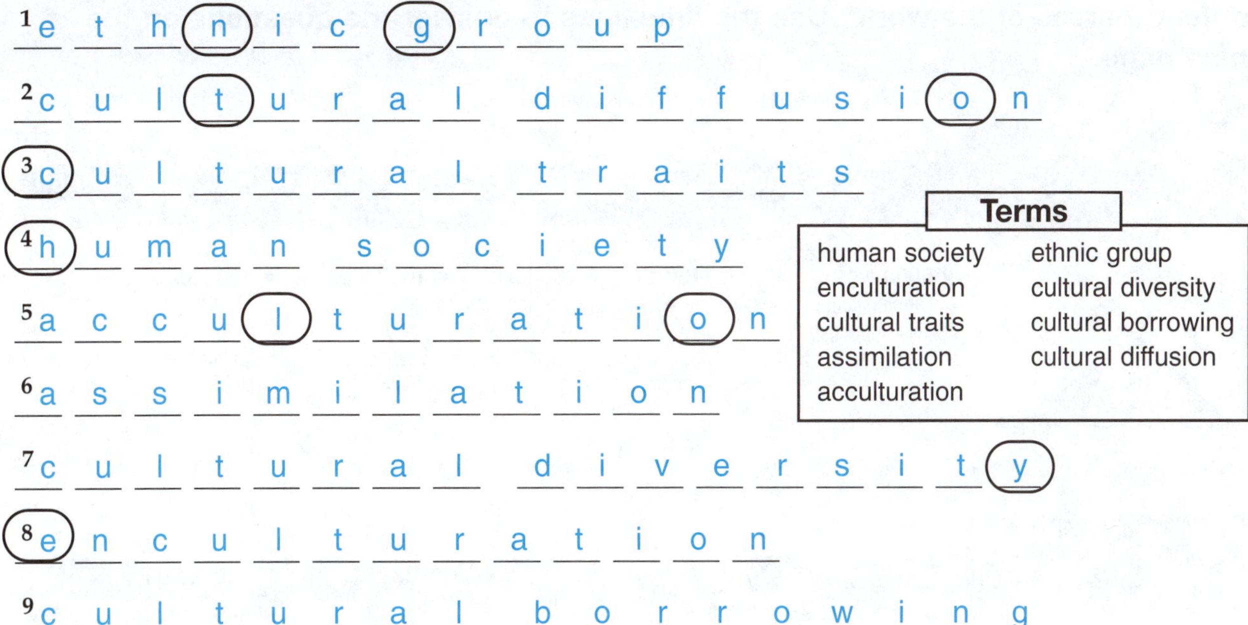

1. e t h n i c g r o u p
2. c u l t u r a l d i f f u s i o n
3. c u l t u r a l t r a i t s
4. h u m a n s o c i e t y
5. a c c u l t u r a t i o n
6. a s s i m i l a t i o n
7. c u l t u r a l d i v e r s i t y
8. e n c u l t u r a t i o n
9. c u l t u r a l b o r r o w i n g

Terms

human society   ethnic group
enculturation   cultural diversity
cultural traits   cultural borrowing
assimilation   cultural diffusion
acculturation

Definitions

1. A group of people who share a culture and way of life are known by this name.
2. Only about ten percent of a society's cultural traits are its own because of this.
3. These are material or nonmaterial characteristics of a society's culture.
4. This is an organized group of people.
5. This happens when two societies have contact for a long time and exchange cultural traits.
6. This happens when immigrants give up their traditions and become part of their new country's culture.
7. This is the result when several ethnic groups live within the same country.
8. Learning national customs is an example of this process.
9. This happens when one society borrows cultural traits from another.

The Internet is the latest example of ___________technology___________ that is spreading cultural traits around the world. At the beginning of the twenty-first century, the United States can be part of a great exchange of world cultures because it has so many computers connected to the Internet. Canada and the countries of Europe and East Asia also have a large presence on the Internet.

CHART AND GRAPH SKILLS
Read Parallel Time Lines

Directions The parallel time line below shows the rise of civilization in three different areas of the world. Use the time lines to answer the questions on the next page.

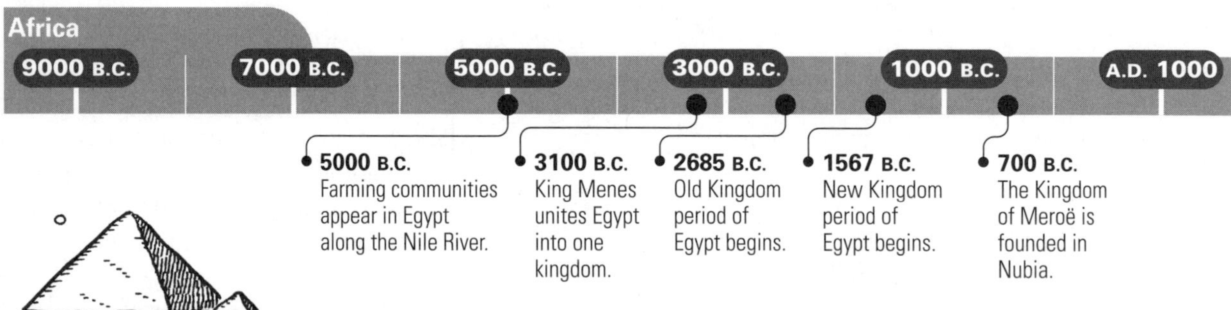

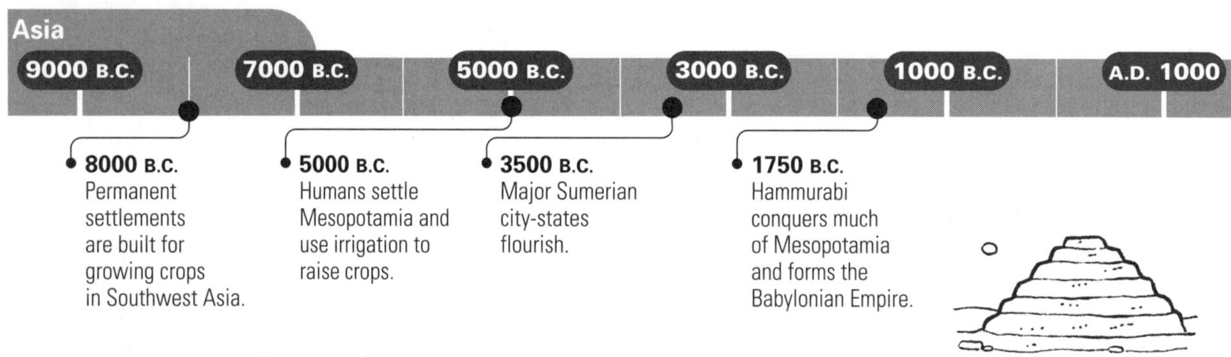

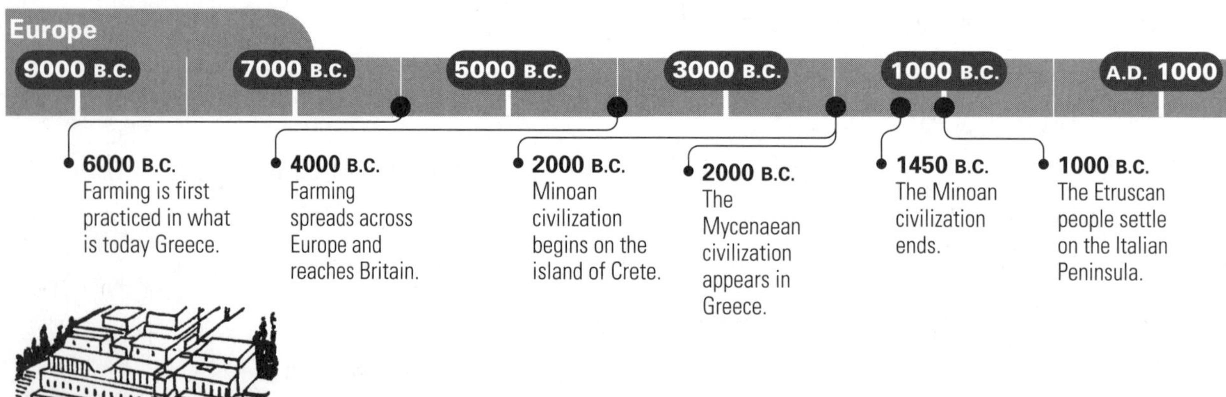

(continued)

Name ____   Date ____________________

1 Where and when was farming first practiced? Southwest Asia, 8000 B.C.

____

2 When was farming first practiced in what is today Greece?

6000 B.C.

3 How many years did it take from the time that farming began in what is today

Greece for it to spread across Europe and reach Britain? It took about 2,000 years

for farming to spread across Europe and reach Britain.

____

4 What happened around 5000 B.C. in Asia and Africa? In Asia, humans settled

the region of Mesopotamia and used irrigation to raise crops. In Africa,

farming communities developed along the Nile River.

5 What civilizations began about 440 years before the New Kingdom period

began in Egypt? The Mycenaean civilization began in Greece and the Minoan

civilization began on the island of Crete.

6 Which country was first united about the same time that the Sumerian city-states

flourished in Asia? Egypt

7 Which African kingdom was founded about 300 years after the Etruscans settled

on the Italian Peninsula? the Kingdom of Meroë

8 Which of these events happened first?
The New Kingdom period began in Egypt.
The Minoan civilization ended.
Hammurabi established the Babylonian Empire.

Hammurabi established the Babylonian Empire first, in 1750 B.C.

____

Governments and Economies

Directions Study the diagram of the different kinds of industry. Use the diagram to help you answer the questions below.

1 Why is the trucking company a tertiary industry? The trucking company is an example of a tertiary industry because it transports harvested wheat from the primary industry and processed cereal from the secondary industry.

2 Which kind of industry is a cereal factory? The cereal factory is a secondary industry, because it turns the wheat into cereal, a finished product.

3 What role does the supermarket have in the sale of the wheat? The supermarket purchases the finished cereal from the cereal factory and sells it to the consumer. The supermarket is considered a business in a tertiary industry, because it sells the finished product of the secondary industry.

4 Does the diagram show the industries of a developed country or a developing country? How do you know? The diagram shows the industries of a developed country. A developed country generally has an established economy with a variety of kinds of industries.

     Use after reading Chapter 2, Lesson 3, pages 68–73.

Looking at Regions

Directions Countries are political regions that can also be divided into smaller regions or subregions. In the United States these subregions are called states. The states can also be divided into smaller regions such as counties and townships. Create a map of the political regions of your home state by following the instructions below.

Students' maps will vary but should include the items listed below.

Draw a map of your state in the box, and label it.

Add major cities and towns to the map.

Find the location of your county in the state.

Draw and label the county.

Add important landforms and bodies of water to the map.

Draw and label an inset map of your city or town.

Locate and label important places related to the community's government.

Locate and label important industries in the community's economy.

CITIZENSHIP SKILLS

Identify National Symbols

Directions Read the paragraph. Then match each flag to the description below. Write the letter of each flag on the line next to the correct description.

Flags are symbols of national identity. Flags can represent a country's people, geography, and culture. Many countries use symbols on their flags to link them to the past. Others use symbols that represent a religion, landforms, or industries found inside their borders. For example, the crescent moon with a star that is found on many flags is an important symbol of the religion of Islam. Some countries use color bars, such as red for courage, to describe their people.

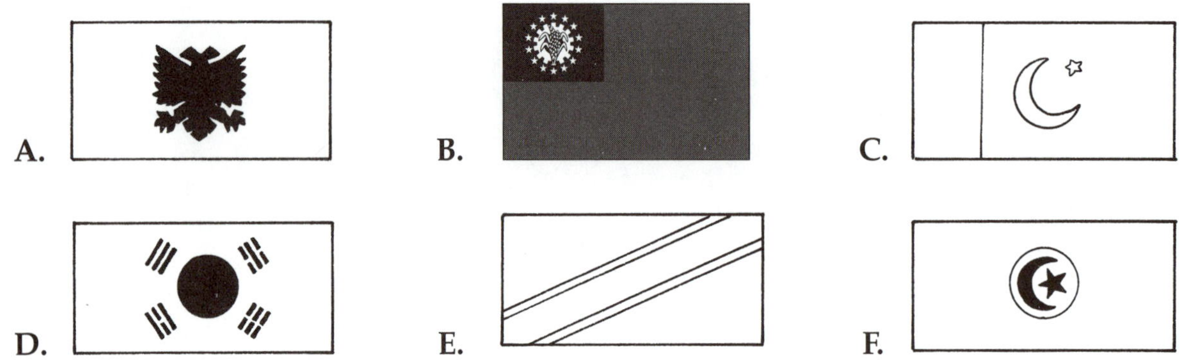

Descriptions

1 __C__ Pakistan's flag has an important Islamic symbol and two colors representing the Muslim majority and the minority groups that live in that country.

2 __D__ One symbol representing equality and four additional symbols representing the four seasons and compass directions are in the middle of the South Korean flag.

3 __E__ Tanzania was formed when two countries, Zanzibar and Tanganyika, united. Tanzania's flag shows two equal pieces joined by a wide bar.

4 __A__ A two-headed eagle sits in the center of Albania's flag, symbolizing this country's history as part of the Byzantine Empire.

5 __F__ The crescent moon and star of Islam are placed in the center of the Tunisian flag.

6 __B__ Myanmar's flag shows a machine wheel and a rice plant to represent industry and agriculture in that country.

Patterns of Life

Directions Complete this graphic organizer to show that you understand how to make generalizations about patterns of settlement.

FACTS + DETAILS	GENERALIZATION

People settle where the climate is mild and the soil is fertile. People also settle in cities to find work. Bodies of water are often near these places.

Students may make generalizations about the effects of climate, landforms, bodies of water, and the availability of work on settlement patterns.

Differences in language, customs, and religion often separate cultures. Contact between cultures, however, spreads cultural ideas. Through technology, people of different cultures can more easily communicate with each other.

Students' generalizations may discuss the role of technology in increasing contact between culture groups, spreading ideas, and bringing cultures closer together.

2 Test Preparation

Directions Read each question and choose the best answer. Then fill in the circle for the answer you have chosen. Be sure to fill in the circle completely.

1 Choose the example of cultural assimilation.
- Ⓐ learning to speak a nation's official language
- Ⓑ practicing an ethnic tradition
- Ⓒ wearing traditional clothing
- Ⓓ forcing religious beliefs on other peoples

2 An example of human adaptation to the environment is—
- Ⓕ building a dam across a river.
- Ⓖ digging the Panama Canal.
- Ⓗ using natural resources to manufacture products.
- Ⓙ wearing heavy sweaters and clothing in a highland climate.

3 Which area has the least concentration of people?
- Ⓐ the Nile valley
- Ⓑ the Arctic Circle
- Ⓒ the Ganges River valley
- Ⓓ the Great European Plain

4 The term *majority rule* means that—
- Ⓕ a person seizes power and makes decisions for all the people.
- Ⓖ decisions are approved by a majority of the people before taking effect.
- Ⓗ a king or queen can make decisions for all the people.
- Ⓙ a group not chosen by the people makes the decisions.

5 Choose the example of a business in a secondary industry.
- Ⓐ a paper factory
- Ⓑ a hospital or doctor's office
- Ⓒ an architectural firm
- Ⓓ a logging company

Use after reading Chapter 2, pages 50–85.

From Sea to Shining Sea

Directions A region is an area of land with parts that share common characteristics. The South is a region with many common characteristics such as landforms, climate, and products. Complete the crossword puzzle to learn some of the South's characteristics. Use your textbook to help you answer the questions below.

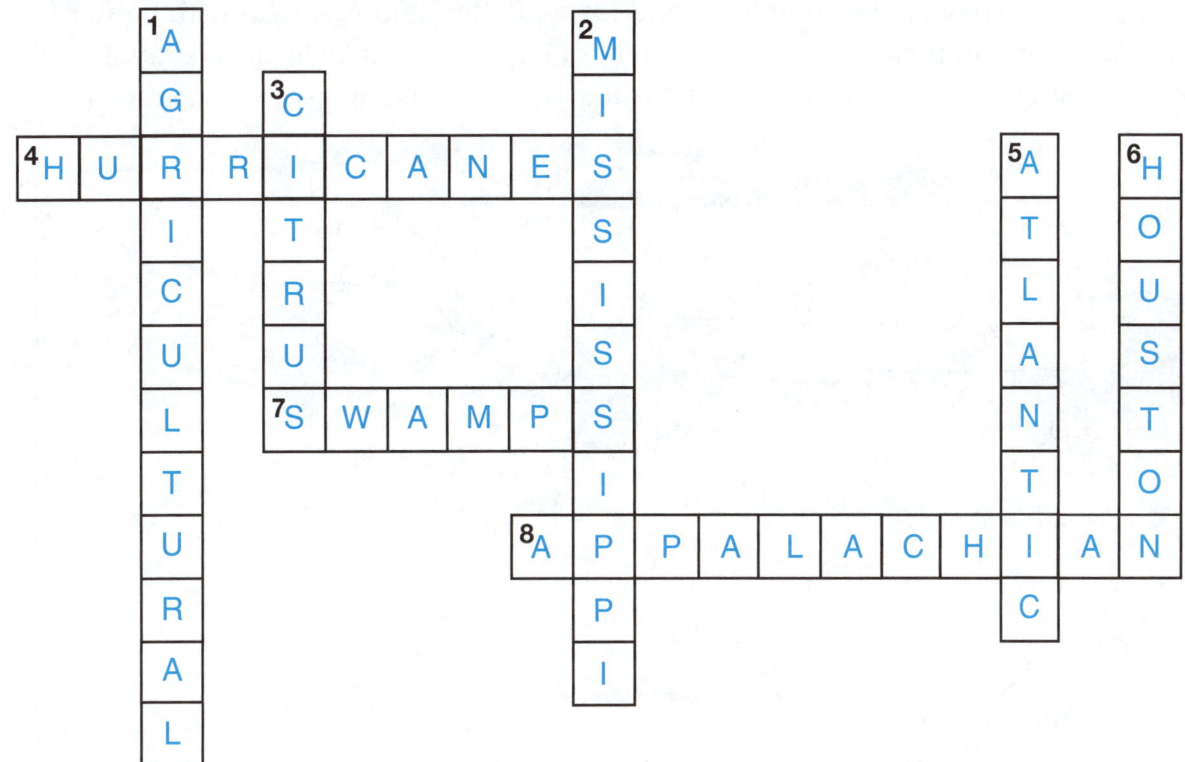

ACROSS

4 From June through November _______ strike the southern coast.

7 The South has many _______, such as the Everglades, which cover 4,000 square miles (about 10,000 sq km) of Florida.

8 The Northeast and the South regions share the _______ Mountains.

DOWN

1 The South is an _______ region because warm temperatures, long summers, and frequent rainfall make it easy to raise crops.

2 The _______ River is an important water highway for travel and trade in the region.

3 The warm climate of the South allows farmers to grow _______ such as oranges and limes.

5 The _______ Coastal Plain is a strip of land that begins in the Northeast and runs along the East and Gulf Coasts.

6 The South is a region of large cities. _______ is one of the large cities and is located in southeastern Texas.

MAP AND GLOBE SKILLS
Read a Relief and Elevation Map

Directions Study the relief and elevation maps below. Use the maps to help you answer the questions that follow on page 29.

A **relief map** shows what kinds of land are located in a region using color or shading. A dark color shows high land, and lower, flatter land is shown with lighter colors. An **elevation map** measures the height of land from sea level. An elevation map uses patterns that connect all the areas that are the same height.

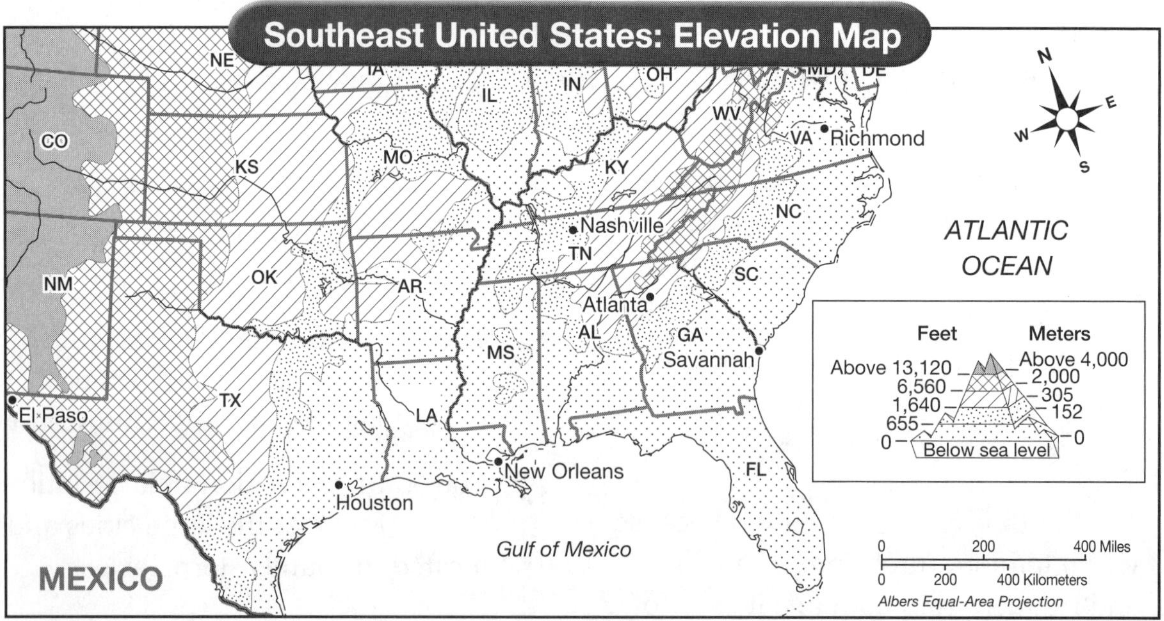

(continued)

     Use after reading Chapter 3, Skill Lesson, pages 104–105.

Name ____ Date _________________________

1 Study the relief map. Which city in Georgia is located on higher land, Savannah

or Atlanta? Atlanta ____

2 Study the elevation map. Which two states are almost entirely at sea level?

Florida and Louisiana ____

3 What is the highest elevation range in the state of North Carolina?

from 6,560 feet (2000 m) above sea level to 13,120 feet (4000 m) above sea level

4 Which city is located on higher land—Nashville, Tennessee, or Houston, Texas?

Nashville, Tennessee ____

Directions Use the maps on page 28 to identify the mystery states. Write the name of the correct state on the line that follows each clue.

5 This state has five areas of elevation. Texas _________________________

6 Which state has the least land at or below 1,640 feet (305 m) above sea level?

Tennessee ____

7 This is the state along the East Coast with the lowest relief.

Florida ____

8 This state is on the East Coast and has three different areas of elevations that range

from sea level to 1,640 feet (305 m) above sea level. South Carolina _________________

A New Republic

Directions Read the paragraph and the list of British laws that led to the American Revolution. Then transport yourself back to 1775, and write a persuasive letter to King George III. Try to persuade the British government to reverse its laws, prevent violence, and grant the colonies representation in Parliament. Use specific laws to make your argument.

In 1763 the French and Indian War ended, leaving Britain in control of almost all of North America. The British Parliament decided that the 13 Colonies should pay for the enormous expense of the war. Over the next ten years, Britain passed several laws that taxed the colonists and restricted their freedom. Many colonists believed that there should not be any laws passed without colonial representation in the British Parliament. Several letters were sent by the colonists to the British government protesting the laws. The letters were ignored. Only protests, violence, and revolution seemed to have any effect.

1764 Sugar Act: Taxed non-British goods entering the colonies.

1765 Quartering Act: Forced the colonies to provide housing for British soldiers.

1765 Stamp Act: Taxed newspapers, almanacs, pamphlets, and other documents.

1766 Declaratory Act: Stated how Parliament could pass any law for the colonies.

1767 Townshend Acts: Taxed glass, lead, paint, paper, and tea.

1772 Tea Act: Cut the taxes on British tea, giving British Tea merchants an unfair advantage over American merchants.

1774 Coercive Acts: Punished Massachusetts for the Boston Tea Party by closing the port of Boston and seizing the colonial government.

1775 New England Restraining Act: Prevented the New England colonies from trading with any other place besides Britain.

Accept all reasonable arguments against taxation without representation and laws restricting colonial freedom. Students' responses should include references to the British laws passed between 1764 and 1775. Students' arguments should also be well structured, with potential solutions to the crisis and statements reinforcing the solutions.

One People, Many Cultures

Directions **Some consider jazz music to be the first original American art. Throughout the 20th century, many musicians experimented with jazz music. Read the biographies of two famous jazz musicians. Then answer the question below.**

Duke Ellington (1899–1974)

Duke Ellington began playing the piano when he was six years old. Ellington did not like the piano and quit until he heard a form of jazz called ragtime. Ragtime was very different from the music that Ellington had studied as a child. He was so impressed by it that he taught himself to play this type of music. Soon Ellington was writing his own music and playing it at high school dances. In the 1920s, he moved to New York City and played with a band. Ellington became famous because his ragtime jazz was different from other artists' music. Ellington added African and Latin music to his arrangements. Over the next few decades, Ellington made records, toured the country, played on American radio shows, and made movies in Hollywood. In 1969, President Nixon awarded Duke Ellington the Presidential Medal of Freedom.

Ella Fitzgerald (1917–1996)

Ella Fitzgerald never had any formal training as a singer and became one of the world's greatest jazz vocalists. Fitzgerald was born in Newport News, Virginia, and by 1934 became a popular singer in New York City. Fitzgerald sang with a swing jazz band that played in many of New York's music clubs. At that time, discrimination made it difficult for African American musicians to perform. Fitzgerald's popularity helped open many doors for other African American musicians. Over the next four decades, she made hundreds of records and sang for many of the great jazz musicians, including Duke Ellington. Fitzgerald won many awards for her music, including 14 Grammy Awards.

What contributions did Ellington and Fitzgerald make to jazz music?

Students' responses may include how Duke Ellington was able to introduce Latin and

African music into ragtime jazz. They may also detail how Ellington was able to bring

his style of jazz to the movies and the radio. Ella Fitzgerald was a skilled jazz singer

who opened new doors for African American musicians. Both individuals helped make

jazz a popular form of music.

READING SKILLS

Determine Point of View

Directions Read the statement below. Answer the questions that follow to determine the point of view of the statement's writer.

Editorials and Opinions

"The American West is a region under siege. It is an area threatened by overpopulation. In the last decade of the twentieth century, millions of Americans have moved to Montana, Idaho, Wyoming, Colorado, and the other states of the American West. In my opinion, the flood of people has been too much for the environment. As more people enter the region, animals are endangered. Entire species of animals are being threatened, as their habitats become new cities and towns. As communities grow, large amounts of forestland are destroyed. To prevent further damage, I believe that we need to put an immediate stop to migration to the American West."

George Smith,
director of the Preserve America's Nature organization

1 How does Mr. Smith feel about the migration of people to the American West?

Mr. Smith believes that migration to the American West should be stopped to

protect the forests and animals of the region.

2 Which words in Mr. Smith's statement help you to determine his point of view?

The words *under siege, threatened, too much*, and *endangered* help to determine

Mr. Smith's point of view.

Directions Imagine that you have just read Mr. Smith's statement in a newspaper. Write a response to Mr. Smith that states an alternate point of view. Continue on another sheet of paper if you need more space.

Responses will vary, but might point out positive aspects of western migration such as

improvements in farming and transportation. Other benefits might include health care,

communication, and democratic government.

Let Freedom Ring

Directions Study the responsibilities of the three branches of the United States government. Decide which branch performs each task. Write the letter of each task under the name of the correct branch name. Use your textbook or a copy of the United States Constitution to help you complete the diagram.

A. Enforces laws

B. Writes and passes laws

C. Decides if the actions of the executive branch are constitutional

D. Creates federal courts

E. Declares war on other countries

F. Leads our country's military

G. Appoints Supreme Court justices and ambassadors

H. Recommends laws

I. Decides if laws are constitutional

J. Approves appointments of Supreme Court justices and ambassadors

K. Amends the Constitution of the United States

L. Approves or vetoes laws

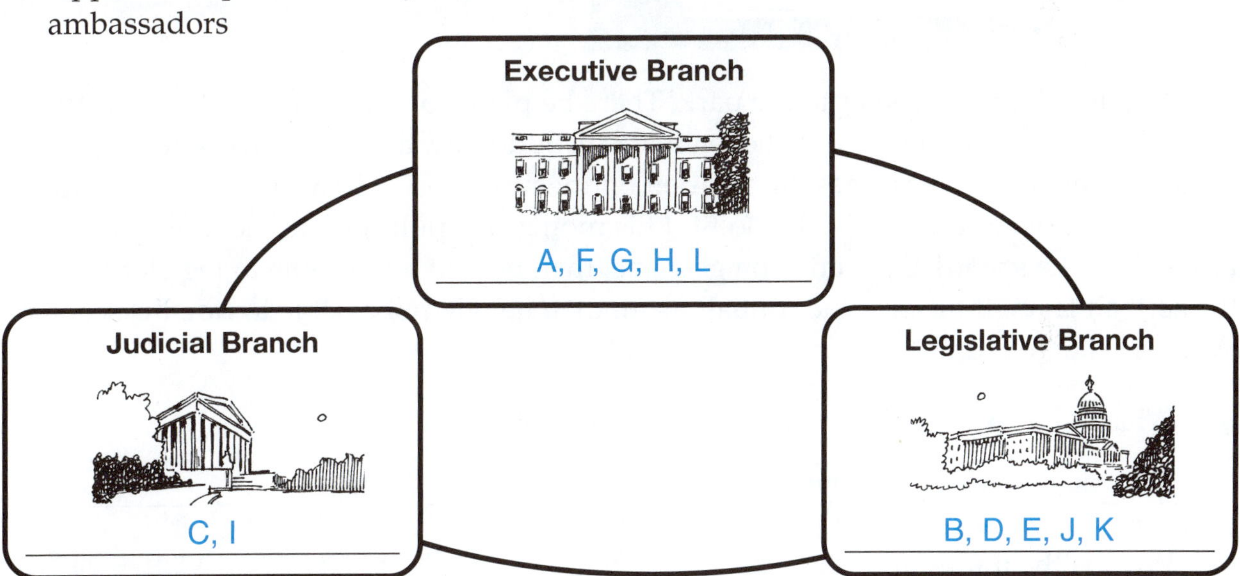

Directions Read the question. Write your answer on the lines provided.

The Constitution of the United States places checks and balances on the power of each of the three branches of government. What are two examples of the checks and balances?

Students' responses may include the executive branch's appointment of Supreme Court justices and ambassadors and the legislature's right of approval. Additional examples include the legislative branch creating laws, the executive branch having veto power, and the judicial branch deciding the constitutionality of the laws.

CITIZENSHIP SKILLS
Make Economic Choices

Directions Making economic choices can be difficult. Scarcity forces us to make trade-offs—giving up one item to get another. Read the paragraph below. Then answer the questions to help Tom make a difficult economic decision.

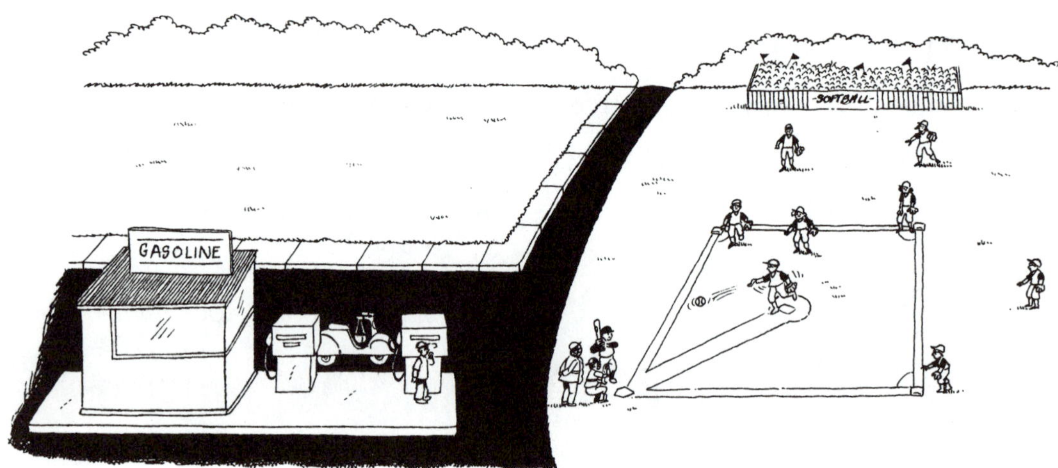

Tom is riding his scooter to the park. There he plans to sign up for the local softball team. The registration fee to join the team is $15. Suddenly, his scooter runs out of gasoline. Luckily, there is a gasoline station on the next block. He walks to the gasoline station and reaches into his pocket to find his money. He pulls out all the money he has—$15. If he spends the money on gasoline, then he will not be able to register for the softball team. If he joins the softball team, then he will not be able to ride his scooter. What should Tom do?

1 What is the example of scarcity in the paragraph above?

the limited amount of money that Tom has

2 What is the trade-off? Tom must decide whether to spend the $15 to buy gasoline

for the scooter or to spend the money to join the softball team.

3 If Tom chooses to buy gasoline for the scooter, what is the opportunity cost of his

economic decision? He loses the chance to join the softball team.

4 What choice would you make? Explain whether you would buy gasoline or join the

softball team. Students' responses may vary.

Name ____ Date ________________________

The United States

 **Directions** Complete this graphic organizer to show that you understand how to summarize key points about the United States.

KEY POINTS  **SUMMARY**

LESSON 1: KEY POINTS

Responses may refer to the four major regions and characteristics that affect population and settlement.

LESSON 1: SUMMARY

Summaries may refer to the four major regions and details about them, including size, population density, climate, growth, and jobs.

LESSON 2: KEY POINTS

Responses may refer to indigenous people living in what is now the United States, British colonists winning independence, the United States as a world leader.

LESSON 2: SUMMARY

Summaries may discuss contact between European settlers and indigenous people, the British colonies, disagreements that led to war and independence, the formation of a democracy, and the United States as a world leader.

LESSON 3: KEY POINTS

Responses may include that the United States is a country of immigrants, that it is like a mosaic, its people share cultural traits, holidays reflect values.

LESSON 3: SUMMARY

Summaries may discuss the United States as a mosaic, people from many countries contributing their ideas, and the ongoing change of culture.

LESSON 4: KEY POINTS

Responses may include that freedom is important, participation by the people, rights and responsibilities of the people, the market economy, the high standard of living in the United States.

LESSON 4: SUMMARY

Summaries may include freedom, the United States economy and government, civic participation, government and citizen responsibilities, and economic freedom.

Name _______________________ Date __________

3 Test Preparation

Directions Read each question and choose the best answer. Then fill in the circle for the answer you have chosen. Be sure to fill in the circle completely.

1 Which of these regions of the United States is the smallest in area but not population?
- Ⓐ the South
- Ⓑ the West
- ● the Northeast
- Ⓓ the Middle West

2 Why do most people in the Northeast live east of the Appalachian Mountains?
- Ⓕ West of the mountains are large plateaus.
- ● The mountains formed a natural barrier to settlers' westward movement.
- Ⓗ The Pacific coastal plain is very narrow and has few harbors.
- Ⓙ The South had many water-filled swamps that slowed settlers' movements.

3 Which of these statements describes a republic?
- Ⓐ The government has three parts that include executive, judicial, and legislative branches.
- Ⓑ All the citizens of the country participate in making and enforcing laws.
- Ⓒ A king or queen leads the country and makes all laws.
- ● The voters choose representatives who make and enforce the laws for them.

4 The federal and state governments share—
- Ⓕ the power to establish an education system.
- Ⓖ the power to form relations with other countries.
- ● the power to make laws.
- Ⓙ the power to make and distribute money.

5 Which statement is an example of a positive social change in recent United States history?
- Ⓐ Immigrants came to the United States and often remained in cities.
- Ⓑ Americans looked to Europe for trends in art, music, and architecture.
- ● Today more women and minorities work in jobs and hold political offices.
- Ⓓ Many Americans faced discrimination and could not own property or vote.

Use after reading Chapter 3, pages 96–131.

Land and the People

Directions Read about one problem facing the Canadian people. Then answer the questions that follow.

Who Can Fish?

Before the arrival of the Europeans, Native Canadians in the Atlantic Provinces and Quebec fished in what are today the waters of the North Atlantic. The Native Canadian fishers harvested lobsters, cod, and other seafood to survive. With the arrival of the Europeans, fishing became an important industry in eastern Canada. Large companies or commercial fisheries harvested millions of tons of fish over the years. In fact so many fish had been harvested by the late twentieth century that the Canadian government declared the region overfished. The government then passed laws to limit the amount of seafood that could be harvested.

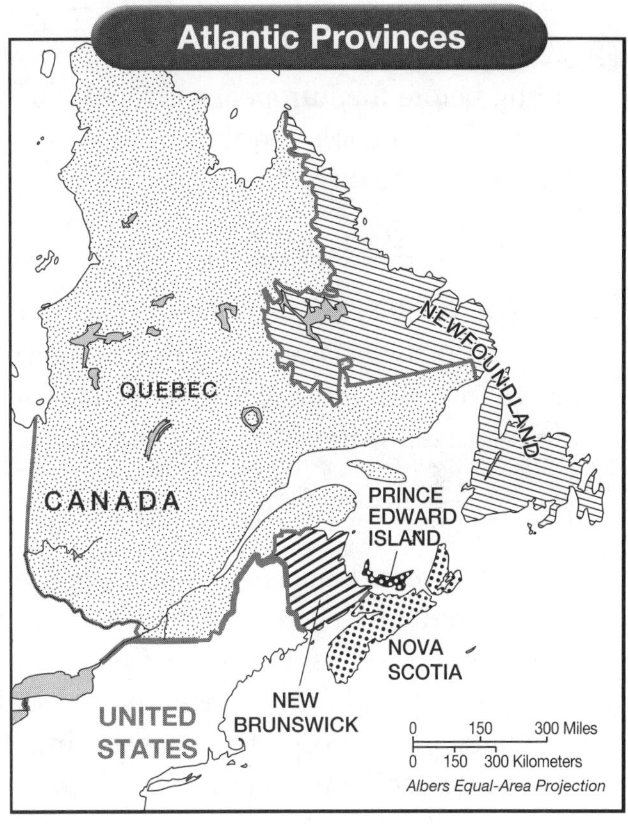

Since the Canadian government's decision to limit fishing, many people in Canada have been affected. Both the Native Canadians and people of European descent who depend on fishing have lost income. Some of the Native Canadians in the region believe that the laws of the Canadian government do not apply to them. They claim that treaties signed by their nations and Canada long ago allow them to continue fishing. Many Native Canadians continue to fish the waters of the North Atlantic. Several people have been arrested for fishing and put on trial by the government.

In 1999 one trial went all the way to Canada's Supreme Court. Canada's highest court ruled that the 34 Native Canadian nations could still fish when and where they wanted. Many Canadians disagreed, and violence broke out. Some Native Canadians found their fishing equipment vandalized. Others were arrested by the Canadian government for overfishing because the laws were not changed.

Fishing is an important industry to the people of Canada. Both Native Canadians and European Canadians in the Atlantic Provinces depend upon it for their livelihood. The Native Canadian nations believe that it is their right to fish as much as they want. Others worry that these nations will overfish the region and destroy the future of the fishing industry.

(continued)

Directions Read the statements. On the line following each statement, write the title of the person who might express such an opinion.

Canadian police officer	Canadian Supreme Court judge
European Canadian fisher	Native Canadian fisher

1 "My people have been fishing in the waters of the North Atlantic for generations. Long before the Europeans arrived, the cod and other seafood gave life to my people. My people cannot be held responsible for overfishing the region and should not be punished for it."

Native Canadian fisher

2 "We have laws in Canada and right now the law states that people can practice only limited fishing. The law applies to everyone. So until that law is changed, we will have to arrest anyone, Native Canadian or European Canadian, who is overfishing in restricted waters."

Canadian police officer

3 "The Supreme Court is giving some Canadians an unfair advantage over others. My community needs to fish and make a living just as those 34 Native Canadian nations. It is unjust that some Canadians be allowed to continue fishing while my community and many more are denied that same right. Besides, if the people of Canada are supposed to be conserving the fish supply, then letting some groups continue fishing will not solve this problem."

European Canadian fisher

4 "The law of Canada above all should be fair—for all Canadians. Throughout history, the government of Canada has signed treaties in good faith with the Native Canadian nations. Our recent fishing laws did not maintain the special relationships we had with the Native Canadians. Our recent fishing laws should not change the rights that Canada granted the Native Canadian nations in earlier treaties. These nations do still have the right to fish in the waters of the North Atlantic."

Canadian Supreme Court judge

5 What do you think about the Canadian fishing crisis in the Atlantic Provinces? Write your opinions in a short paragraph below. You may use a separate sheet of paper.

Students' responses may include that the laws limiting the amount of fishing

(for Native Canadians and/or European Canadians) are unfair. Others may

agree that the Native Canadians should be allowed to continue fishing.

     Use after reading Chapter 4, Lesson 1, pages 134–141.

Through the Centuries

Directions Below are products of two different early groups that settled in Canada. Read each description, and study the drawings. Use the drawings to answer the questions and describe the groups that made these products.

Canada's first people were the Native Canadians who crossed a land bridge from Asia sometime between 12,000 and 40,000 years ago. Some settled in the deep forests of the southeast and the west coast. Others settled the rocky Canadian Shield, the cold northern territories, and the flat, treeless Interior Plains. The Native Canadians used whatever resources the regions had to offer in order to survive. We can study the products they left behind to learn about the regions they lived in and how they used resources to survive.

**Assiniboine tepee, shoe, and tool
made from the American bison**

**Nootka canoe, tool, and house
made from many resources**

1 What do the Assiniboine products show about the region of Canada in which that group lived? The Assiniboine products show that the group lived in a region where bison were plentiful. The products also tell us that wood was not as plentiful as in other regions of Canada.

2 What do the Assiniboine products show about that group and how it used natural resources? The Assiniboine products show that the group was mobile and lived in semipermanent homes. They also show that the group used all the resources the region had to offer and did not waste much of its most plentiful resource, the bison.

3 In what type of region did the Nootka people live? How did the Nootka use the resources of its region to survive? The Nootkas lived in an area close to forests and the ocean. They used the region's resources to build shelter for protection and tools for hunting. The Nootkas used the forests' wood for homes and canoes, seashells for tools such as harpoons, and other ocean products such as sealskin.

Canada's Government

Directions **Hold an election to set up a classroom government that is based on the Canadian parliamentary system. Study the chart below and carefully read the instructions. Follow each step to elect your class leaders.**

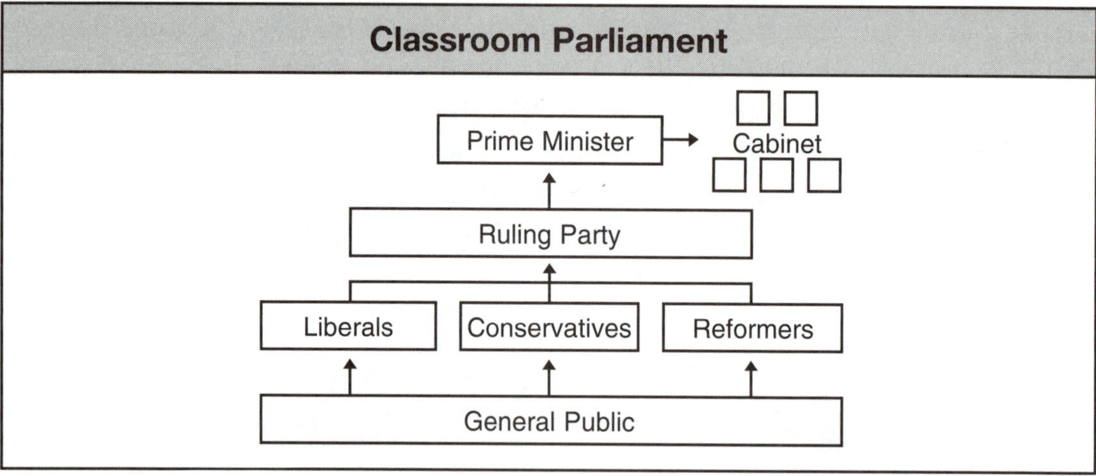

1 As a class, divide into four groups: Liberals, Conservatives, Reformers, and general public. The members of the three political parties are all candidates for the position of Member of Parliament, or MP.

2 Everyone should vote for one candidate. Fill in the name of your candidate on a piece of paper and pass your ballot to your teacher.

3 Tally the votes and announce the names of the candidates who received votes. All the candidates who received votes have seats in the classroom Parliament.

4 Total each political party's MPs. The party with the most elected MPs controls the classroom Parliament as the ruling party.

5 The MPs of the ruling party should choose a leader, or a prime minister. The prime minister must choose five cabinet members to advise him or her about classroom laws. The prime minister can only choose the ministers from the elected MPs.

Directions **Answer the question below. Write your answer on the lines provided.**

6 Describe two ways that a parliamentary election is different from an election in the United States. Students' responses may include the addition of several political parties in the process, the indirect selection of the prime minister by the ruling party and not by the voters, and the idea that the prime minister can select Cabinet members only from elected MPs.

CHART AND GRAPH SKILLS

Follow a Flow Chart

Directions Study the flow chart. Then use the information in the flow chart to answer the questions on the following page.

The School Budget Process

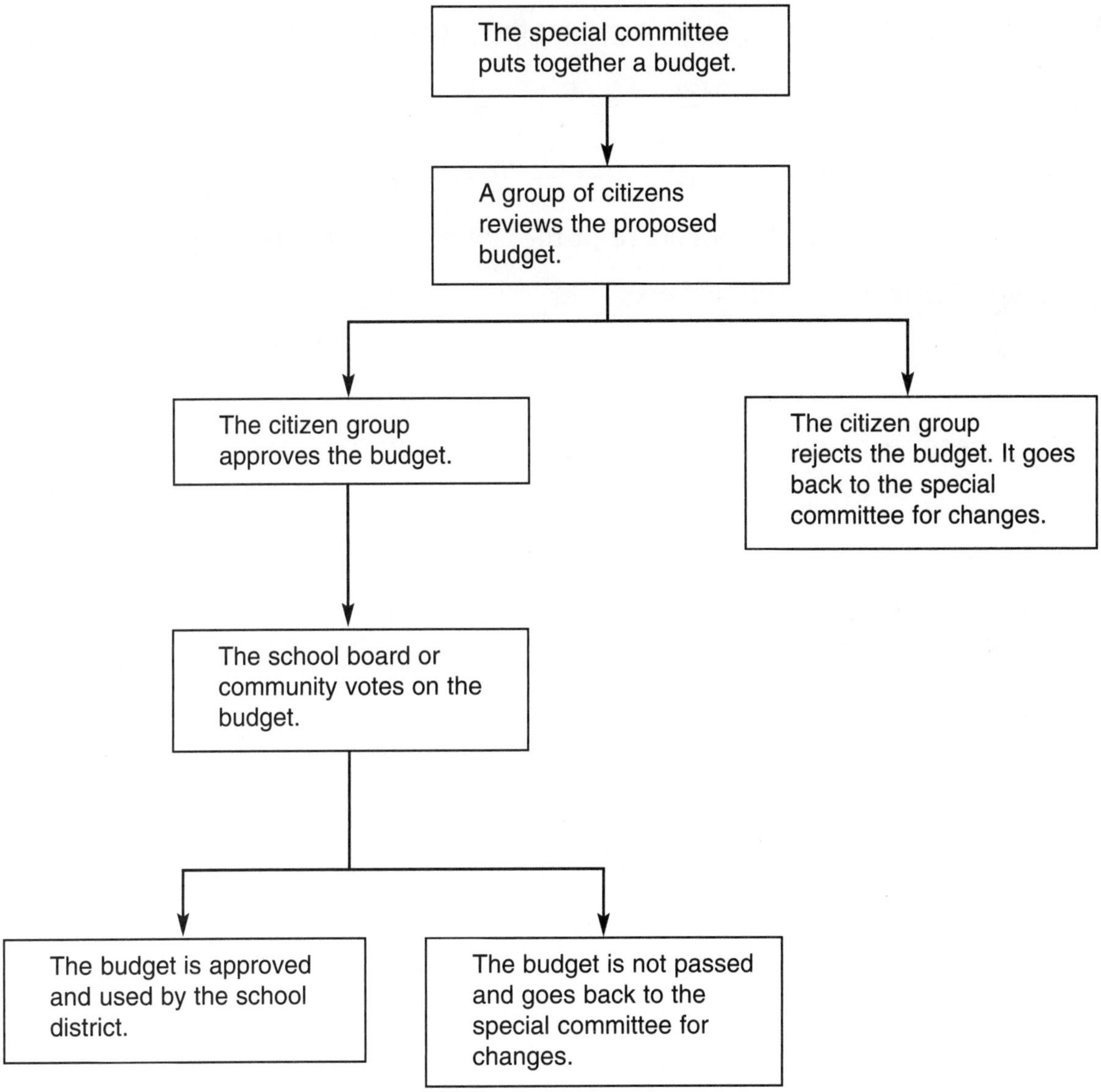

The special committee puts together a budget.

↓

A group of citizens reviews the proposed budget.

The citizen group approves the budget.

The citizen group rejects the budget. It goes back to the special committee for changes.

The school board or community votes on the budget.

The budget is approved and used by the school district.

The budget is not passed and goes back to the special committee for changes.

(continued)

Use after reading Chapter 4, Skill Lesson, pages 154–155.

Name ____ Date ___________________________

1 What is the process that is being explained on page 41?

how a school district gets its budget

2 Which group is the first to review the special committee's proposed budget?

a group of citizen reviewers

3 What happens if the citizen group approves the proposed budget?

The school board or the entire community votes to approve the budget.

4 What happens next if the school board or the community does not approve the

budget? The budget is sent back to the special committee to be changed.

5 What happens next if the school board or the community approves the budget?

The budget is used by the school district.

6 What part of a flow chart tells you about the process that is being explained in

the chart? the title of the flow chart

7 What part of a flow chart shows you that the steps are linked?

The arrows between the steps show that they are linked.

8 Which parts of the process are shown in the ovals or boxes of a flow chart?

the steps in a process

Canada

Directions Complete this graphic organizer to show that you understand how to draw conclusions about Canada based on what you read and what you already know.

WHAT YOU READ	 WHAT YOU KNOW	 CONCLUSION
People living in Canada have settled in places with fertile soil and access to water. They use natural resources from northern Canada but live in the south where the climate is warmer.	It is hard to live in places where the weather is cold and where the mountainous land is covered with thick forests.	Much of northern Canada is uninhabited or has few people living there because of its climate and landforms.
Canadians elect representatives, but their prime minister is chosen by the ruling party from among these representatives. Canada's federal system divides power between its national government and its provinces.	**Every country has its own form of government. The government of the United States is a democracy. People elect officials and no one branch of government has absolute power.**	Canada's system of government is based on Great Britain's, but has been adapted to suit its particular needs.

4 Test Preparation

Name _______________________ Date ___________

Directions Read each question and choose the best answer. Then fill in the circle for the answer you have chosen. Be sure to fill in the circle completely.

1 Which region has frozen soil, ice, and is the least likely to provide Canadians with fertile farmland?
- Ⓐ Appalachian region
- **Ⓑ** Arctic Islands region
- Ⓒ St. Lawrence Lowlands region
- Ⓓ Interior Plains region

2 In the Canadian government, the official with the smallest role is—
- Ⓕ the Speaker of the House of Commons.
- Ⓖ the prime minister.
- **Ⓗ** the king or queen of Britain.
- Ⓙ a Member of Parliament.

3 Unlike the President of the United States, the Canadian prime minister is not chosen by the people. He or she is—
- Ⓐ selected by the king or queen of Britain.
- **Ⓑ** chosen by the MPs of the ruling party.
- Ⓒ elected by the Supreme Court.
- Ⓓ chosen by the leaders of the provinces.

4 Which Native Canadian group survived by creating products from the American bison?
- Ⓕ Ottawa
- Ⓖ Huron
- Ⓗ Inuit
- **Ⓙ** Assiniboine

5 What was the effect of Giovanni Caboto's search for a northern water route to Asia?
- **Ⓐ** The English claimed the land of Newfoundland.
- Ⓑ The English claimed all the land around the St. Lawrence River.
- Ⓒ The Vikings explored Canada but returned to Scandinavia.
- Ⓓ The French founded the colony of New France.

Use after reading Chapter 4, pages 132–157.

A Rugged Land

Directions Mexico is a land of steep mountains, hot deserts, and high plateaus. It also has three climate and vegetation regions: the tierra caliente, the tierra templada, and the tierra fría. Study the cross-section of this rugged land. Use the cross-section to answer the questions that follow.

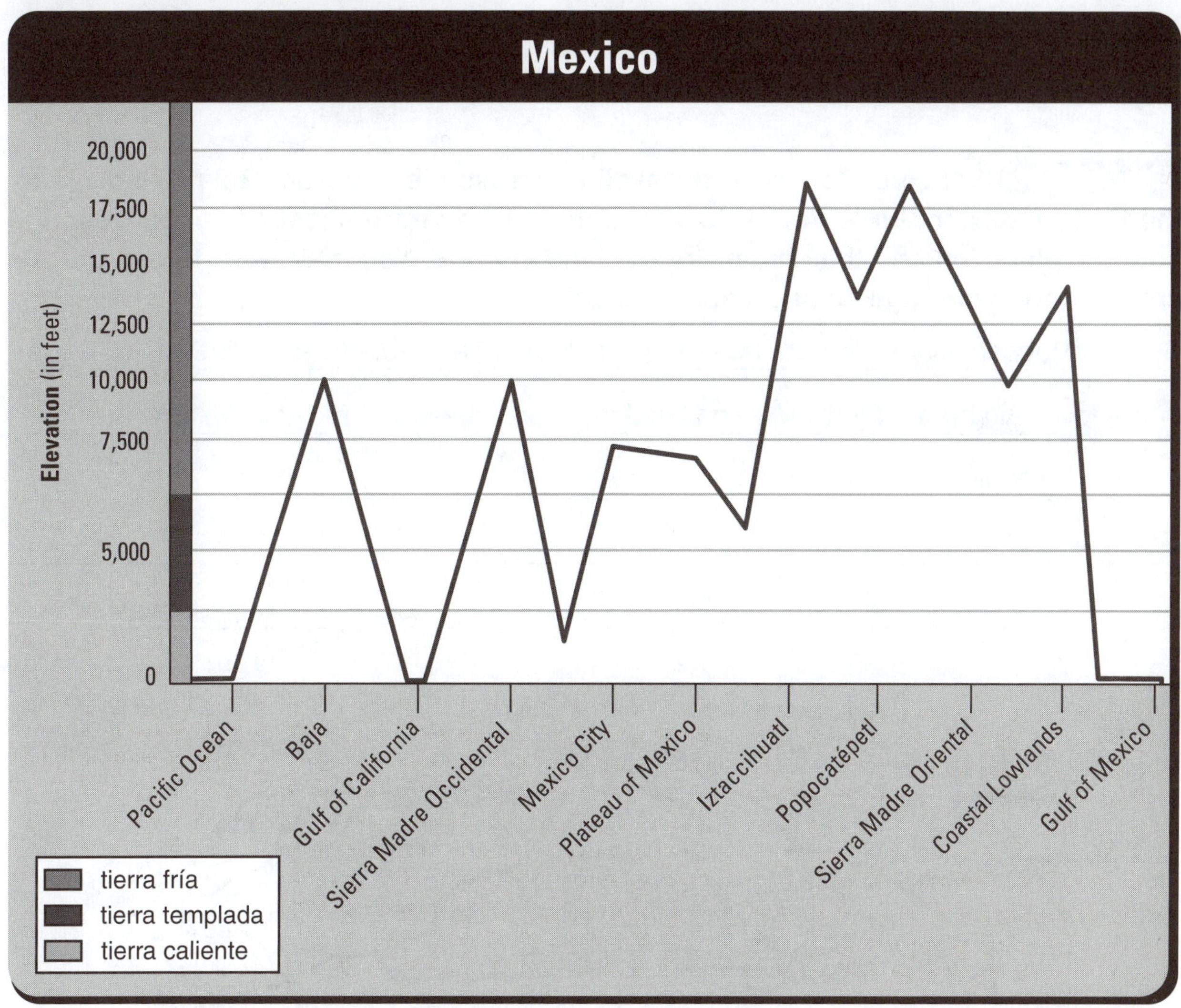

1 Into which climate and vegetation zone does the volcano Popocatépetl reach?

tierra fría

2 What is the average height of the Plateau of Mexico? approximately 7,000 feet

3 Into which climate and vegetation zone does the land next to the Gulf of Mexico fall? tierra caliente

4 At how many feet above sea level is Mexico City located? approximately 7,350

(continued)

Directions Below are the names of six cities, landforms, and bodies of water found in Mexico. Number them 1–6 in the correct order of elevation, using 1 for the lowest and 6 for the highest feature. Use the cross-section on page 45 to help you complete the activity.

3	Mexico City	2	Plateau of Mexico
6	Iztaccíhuatl	5	Sierra Madre Oriental
1	Gulf of California	4	Sierra Madre Occidental

Directions Imagine that you are traveling across Mexico from Baja California to the Gulf of Mexico. Write your observations on a separate sheet of paper. Describe how the elevation and the climate of the land change. You may want to use the cross-section on page 45 and your textbook.

Students' observations will vary but should include details about traveling through some of the following areas: Sierra Madre Occidental, the Plateau of Mexico, Mexico City, and the coastal lowlands.

   Use after reading Chapter 5, Lesson 1, pages 172–176.

Creating a Mexican Culture

Directions Read the following paragraphs about the city of Tenochtitlán. Then number the illustrations to show the order of events in the city's growth.

The capital of the Aztec Empire was a fabulous city called Tenochtitlán. Although the settlement eventually became one of Earth's largest cities, it had very simple beginnings. In 1325 the Aztecs came to the Valley of Mexico and claimed an island in the middle of Lake Texcoco. The island had poor soil, and few crops could grow there. To solve this problem, the Aztecs built floating gardens called *chinampas* on the lake.

The Aztecs built these floating gardens by first making large rafts from the reeds that grew along the lake. The rafts were covered with many layers of mud and were anchored to the lake floor with large poles. Then seeds were planted in the layers of mud. As the plants grew, their roots reached down into the lake water. On some rafts, the Aztecs planted willow trees to hold the soil and keep it from blowing or washing away.

The Aztec harvests were plentiful, and the floating gardens grew larger. The Aztecs then began to fill in the spaces between the chinampas in the same way. There they built homes, shops, and temples. Eventually, the settlement grew to include other small islands in Lake Texcoco. Large causeways were built to connect the growing city to the mainland and the other islands. Later the Aztecs would extend their rule to areas beyond Lake Texcoco, but the city of Tenochtitlán would always remain the empire's largest and most powerful city.

3 _______

2 _______

1 _______

Name ____ Date ___________________

Yesterday and Today

Directions A glossary is a list of specialized words and their definitions. It is found in many of the books you read. Sometimes a glossary includes historical or geographical terms and even some biographical information. Below is a glossary with the definitions missing. Complete it by filling in the definitions. You may want to use your textbook to help you.

C

Constitution of 1917 The Mexican constitution that returned land to poor farmers and established a presidential democracy with the president as the country's chief decision maker.

D

Díaz, Porfirio A general in the Mexican army who named himself president and seized control of the government in 1876.

F

Federal District Mexico City and its surrounding territory.

G

General Congress Mexico's national legislature, which is made up of the Senate and the Chamber of Deputies.

H

Hidalgo, Miguel A Catholic priest whose 1810 speech urged Mexicans to rebel against Spain and fight for independence.

I

Institutional Revolutionary Party Mexico's leading political party, which controlled the government and presidency from 1929 until 2000.

J

Juárez, Benito The president of Mexico who attempted to pass laws limiting the power of the Catholic Church, reforming elections, and educating the Mexican people.

                Use after reading Chapter 5, Lesson 3, pages 183–187.

READING SKILLS

Identify Cause and Effect

Directions Read the paragraphs below about Benito Juárez, the Mexican War of Reform, and Maximilian, the Austrian prince who became Mexico's emperor. Then use the information in the paragraphs to complete the activities on page 50.

In 1857 a group of Mexicans known as the Liberals took control of the Mexican government. They estabised a new constitution, limited the president's power and that of the Catholic Church, and set up regular elections. Many Mexicans in the army and in the Catholic Church, as well as wealthy landowners, were not happy with these changes. They decided to overthrow the government, forcing the Mexican president and his cabinet to flee.

Benito Juárez, the Chief Justice of the Supreme Court, decided to resist. He declared himself President of Mexico and set up his capital at Veracruz. As a result the civil war known as the War of Reform began. By 1861 Juárez's army had seized Mexico City. In 1862 France, Britain, and Spain sent military forces to Mexico to secure repayment of debts from Juárez's government. They soon occupied the port of Veracruz.

Maximilian 1832–1867

The French, however, had another plan. The French Emperor Napoleon III wanted to set up a new French Empire in Mexico. He sent a large army to Mexico, marched to Mexico City, and seized the capital. Then Napoleon placed an Austrian prince named Maximilian on the throne of Mexico.

Maximilian became the Emperor of Mexico in 1864, but only a few Mexicans recognized his rule. Most saw the French forces as invaders and Maximilian as a puppet ruler. Juárez and his army continued to fight the French. After years of fighting, Napoleon decided to pull the French army out of Mexico in 1867. Without the French to protect him, Maximilian was captured in a battle at the town of Querétaro. Soon after, Maximilian was put on trial, found guilty of treason, and executed. Juárez's army quickly retook control of Mexico City and the entire country.

(continued)

Directions Study the diagram below. Fill in the missing causes and effects with information from the story of the War of Reform on page 49.

CAUSES → EFFECTS

The Mexican president and cabinet flee when the government is overthrown.

The War of Reform begins. _______________

Benito Juárez and his army

seize control of Mexico City.

The governments of France, Britain, and Spain fear that Juárez's government will not repay its debts.

The French send an army to Mexico and take control of Mexico City.

Maximilian becomes Emperor

of Mexico.

Napoleon decides to pull the

French army out of Mexico.

Juárez captures Maximilian and takes control of Mexico.

Name _________________________________ Date _____________

Mexico

Directions Complete this graphic organizer to show that you understand how to compare and contrast different groups and cultures, such as the Olmecs and the Maya.

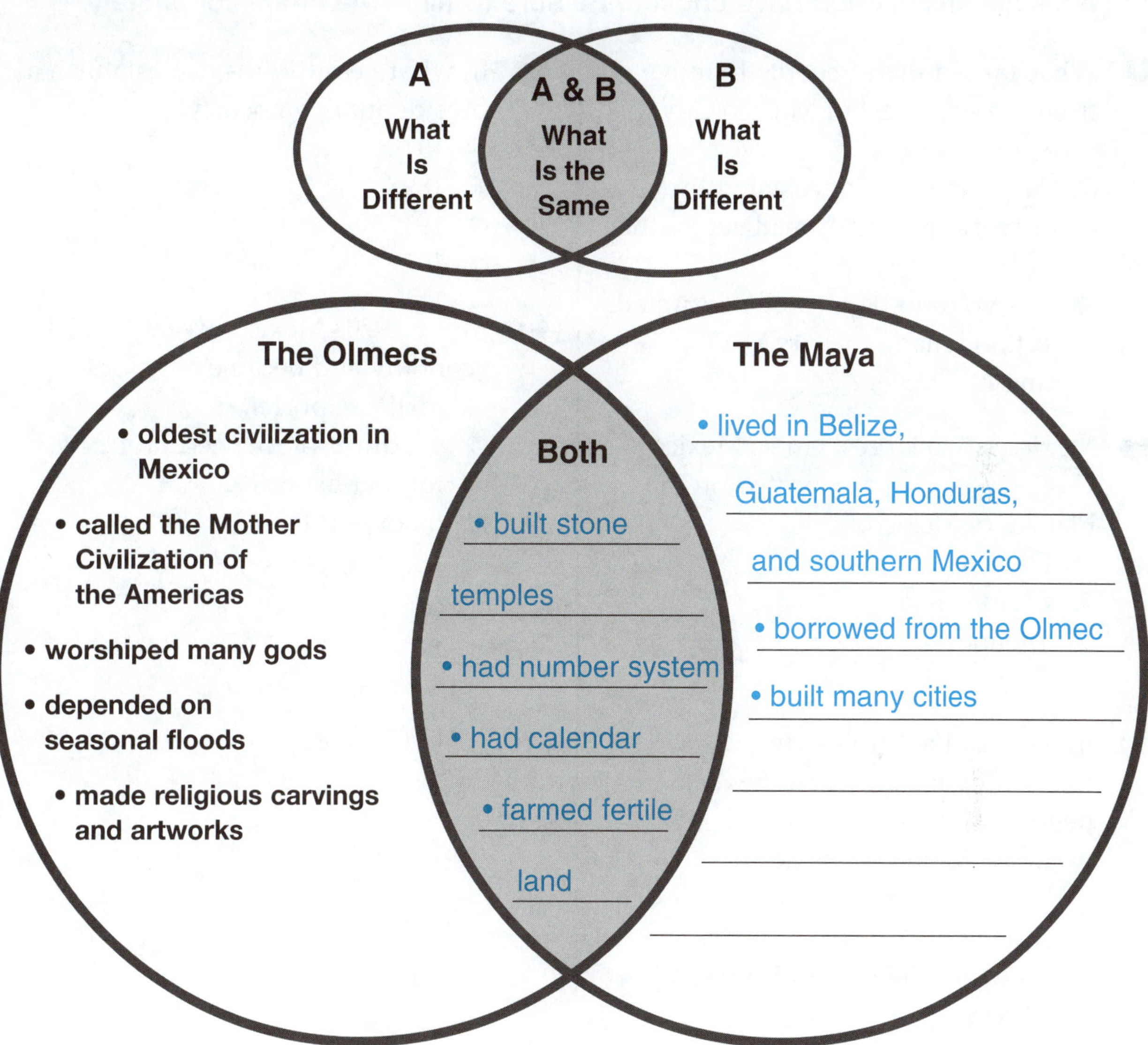

Name _________________________ Date __________

Test Preparation

1 What caused many people to move from the southeast of Mexico City in 1996?
- Ⓐ An earthquake devastated the city.
- Ⓑ A great drought spread across the land.
- **Ⓒ** The volcano Popocatépetl erupted.
- Ⓓ A flood made the city uninhabitable.

2 Mexico's two largest cities, Mexico City and _______, are located on the Plateau of Mexico.
- Ⓕ Baja
- **Ⓖ** Guadalajara
- Ⓗ Tijuana
- Ⓙ Tikal

3 In the A.D. 1200s the Aztec civilization began when the Aztec people settled—
- **Ⓐ** in the Valley of Mexico.
- Ⓑ on the coast of the Gulf of Mexico.
- Ⓒ in the rain forests of Belize.
- Ⓓ on the Pacific coast of western Mexico.

4 In what year did Mexico establish a presidential democracy?
- Ⓕ 1910
- Ⓖ 1898
- **Ⓗ** 1917
- Ⓙ 1922

5 In the 1970s Mexico diversified its economy and became a major—
- Ⓐ textile exporter.
- Ⓑ producer of finished products.
- Ⓒ lumber exporter.
- **Ⓓ** oil exporter.

Use after reading Chapter 5, pages 170–191.

Mountains, Volcanoes, Islands, and Hurricanes

Directions Middle America has many special geographical features, such as cays, straits, and forests. Study the terms in the box below. Some are terms you learned in your textbook. Others you learned before. Label each of the pictures below with one of the terms from the box.

archipelago	cay	coastal lowland	coniferous trees	coral reef
isthmus	peninsula	strait	trade winds	volcano

1  coral reef

6  cay

2  isthmus

7  coastal lowland

3  strait

8  archipelago

4  trade winds

9  coniferous trees

5  volcano

10 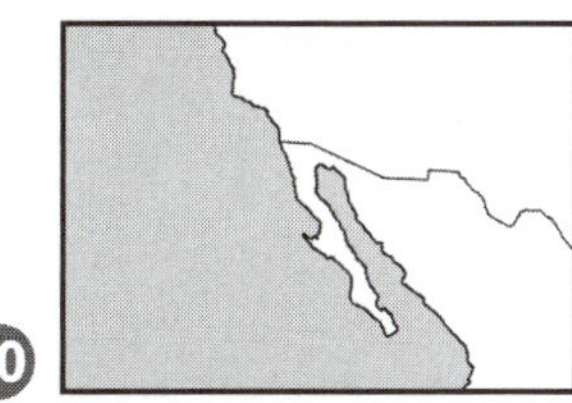 peninsula

(continued)

Name ____ Date ______________________

11 The two subregions that make up Middle America are

___________Central America___________ and the Caribbean.

12 A ___________cay___________ is a small, low-lying island made of sand, limestone, or coral.

13 In the mountainous areas of Central America, there are many cone-bearing

evergreen trees called ___________coniferous trees___________.

14 Winds that consistently blow from northeast of the Caribbean toward the equator

are called the ___________trade winds___________.

15 The chain of islands in the Caribbean is an ___________archipelago___________.

16 A hard, stony material made from the skeletons of sea animals is called

___________coral___________.

17 At the southernmost tip of Central America is a narrow strip of land, called an

___________isthmus___________, that separates the Atlantic and Pacific Oceans.

18 The ___________coastal lowland___________ areas located along the Central American coast have a tropical climate with plenty of rain.

19 The ash from erupting ___________volcanoes___________ keeps Central America's soil fertile.

20 Cuba is the largest ___________island___________ in the Caribbean archipelago.

   Use after reading Chapter 6, Lesson 1, pages 194–199.

Influences of the Past

Directions Many ethnic groups settled in Central America and the Caribbean. Read each of the descriptions below. Draw lines connecting the group descriptions and the correct group names below. There may be more than one line from a description or to a group.

1 Scientists believe this group was the first to settle on the Caribbean islands.

Arawaks

Ciboneys

2 These three different ethnic groups lived in the Caribbean region during the 1300s and the 1400s.

Caribs

3 These colonists began settling on the islands of the Caribbean in the early 1600s.

English

French

4 The people of this civilization built more than 100 cities in present-day Belize, El Salvador, Guatemala, and Honduras.

Dutch

Maya

5 This group of colonists forced the Arawaks to work as slaves on large plantations.

Spanish

Directions On a separate sheet of paper, write a short paragraph that explains how the Dutch, English, French, and Spanish influenced the people that lived in the region.

Responses should discuss how Europeans conquered and enslaved people,

but also added to native cultures.

(continued)

Directions Read the sentences below and decide if they are true or false. Label the sentences *T* if they are true or *F* if they are false. Rewrite the false sentences to make them true.

6. __F__ In 1492, Christopher Columbus, an explorer sailing for France, landed in the Bahamas.

In 1492, Christopher Columbus, an explorer sailing for Spain, landed in the Bahamas.

7. __T__ By the early 1600s, colonists from Europe were starting settlements in the Caribbean region.

8. __F__ The English and the French did not get their plantation workers from the African slave trade. The English and the French did get their plantation workers from the African slave trade.

9. __T__ As sugar production in the Caribbean grew in the 1700s, so did the number of Africans in the Caribbean population.

10. __F__ In some places in the Caribbean region, slavery was abolished because the price of tobacco fell. In some places in the Caribbean region, slavery was abolished because the price of sugar fell.

11. __F__ The Aztecs built more than 100 cities in what are today Belize, El Salvador, Guatemala, and Honduras. The Maya built more than 100 cities in what are today Belize, El Salvador, Guatemala, and Honduras.

12. __F__ The Spanish arrived in Central America in the 1700s.

The Spanish arrived in Central America in the 1500s.

                    Use after reading Chapter 6, Lesson 2, pages 200–205.

Contrasts in Governing

Directions Read the descriptions of political events below and write the date when each event occurred. Then write the number of the event in the correct place under the time line below. You may want to use your textbook to help you figure out the correct dates.

1 _____1823_____ The Central American countries form a federation called the United Provinces of Central America.

2 _____1903_____ Panama wins independence from Colombia.

3 _____1987_____ Oscar Arias Sanchez wins the Nobel Peace Prize for creating a Central American peace plan.

4 _____1821_____ Costa Rica, El Salvador, Guatemala, Honduras, and Nicaragua win independence from Spain.

5 _____1981_____ Belize becomes an independent country.

6 _____1804_____ Haiti wins independence from France.

7 _____1917_____ The United States purchases the Virgin Islands from Denmark.

8 _____1959_____ Fidel Castro and his supporters create a Communist government in Cuba.

Contrasts in Governing

1800	1825	1850	1875	1900	1925	1950	1975	2000

1804 — 1821 — 1823 — 1903 — 1917 — 1959 — 1981 — 1987

6   4   1   2   7   8   5   3

CITIZENSHIP SKILLS
Make a Thoughtful Decision

Directions **Imagine you are a citizen of Puerto Rico preparing to vote on whether the island should remain a commonwealth or become the 51st state of the United States. Read the paragraph below. Then make a thoughtful decision by writing a brief paragraph to answer the questions that follow.**

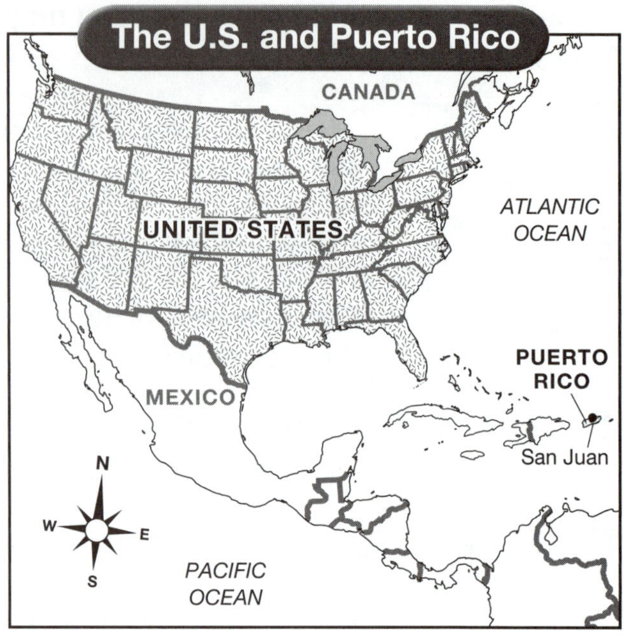

In 1952, the people of Puerto Rico adopted a constitution that created the Commonwealth of Puerto Rico. As inhabitants of a United States territory Puerto Ricans are citizens of the United States and share most of the rights of other United States citizens. For example, the people of Puerto Rico cannot vote for the President or members of Congress and have little say in the creation of the country's national laws. On the positive side, citizens of Puerto Rico maintain their heritage and do not pay federal income taxes.

• What is an advantage of remaining a commonwealth?

• What is a disadvantage of remaining a commonwealth?

• Will you vote for Puerto Rico to become a state? Why?

Students' responses will vary but should include some of the following: An advantage of Puerto Rico remaining a commonwealth is that its culture will be protected. A disadvantage is that the people of Puerto Rico will continue to have only limited rights of citizenship. There are many benefits of statehood, and much of Puerto Rico's culture would be preserved anyway. That's why becoming a state seems more important.

Central America and the Caribbean

Directions Complete the graphic organizer below to show that you understand the sequence of events that ended Spanish control of Central America and led to the creation of independent countries there. Complete the next organizer to show that you understand the order of events that caused enslaved Africans to be brought to the Caribbean.

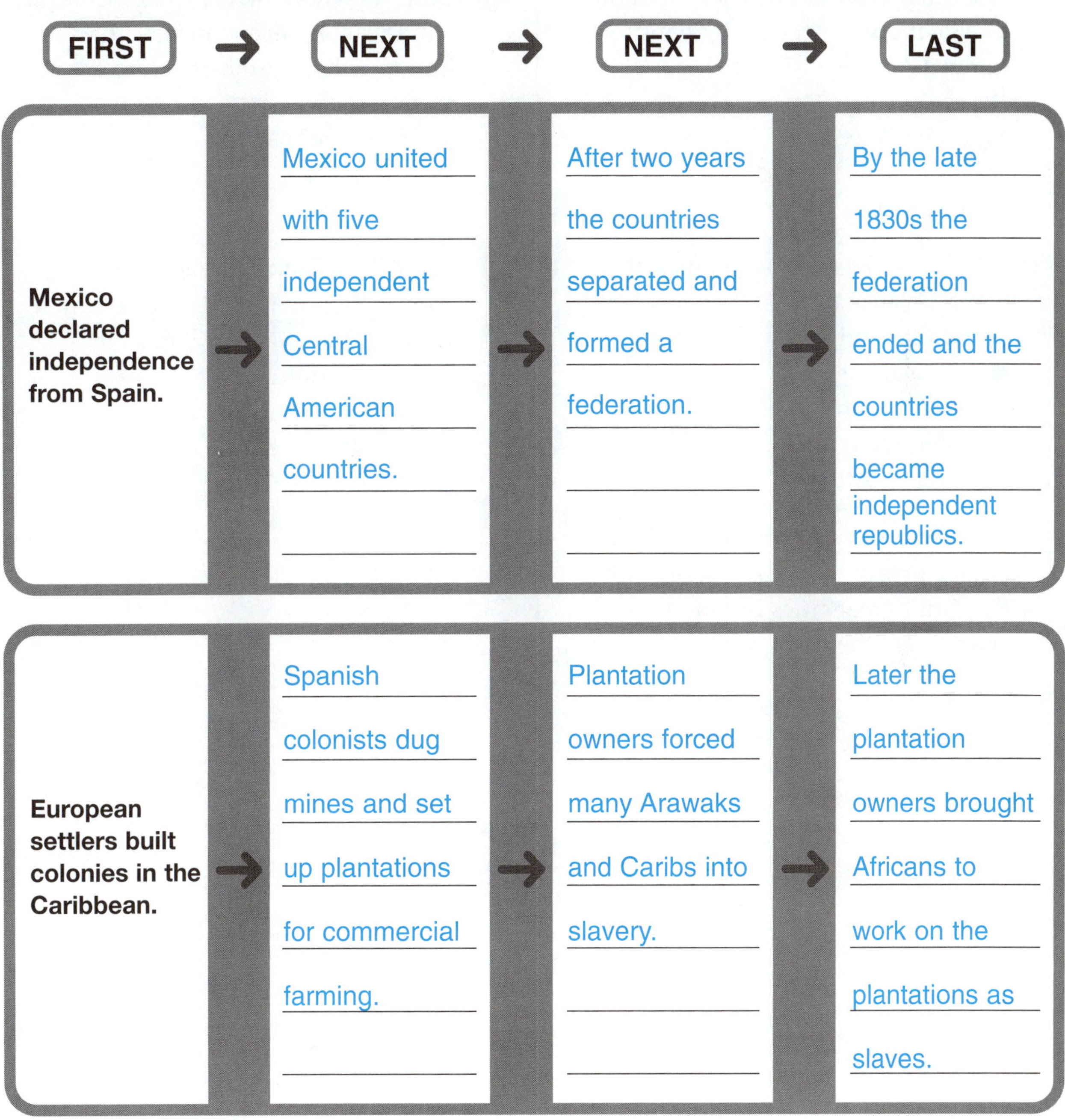

6 Test Preparation

Name _________________________ Date _________

1 The most successful crop grown on the Pacific and Atlantic lowlands of Central America is—
- Ⓐ coffee.
- Ⓑ sugarcane.
- Ⓒ corn.
- Ⓓ bananas.

2 The ______ Islands were given their name because they are sheltered from the trade winds.
- Ⓕ Leeward
- Ⓖ Lesser Antilles
- Ⓗ Windward
- Ⓙ Greater Antilles

3 What was the name of the ancient civilization of Central America that built great cities but later abandoned them?
- Ⓐ Maya
- Ⓑ Inca
- Ⓒ Olmec
- Ⓓ Aztec

4 Leaders who took control of Central American governments and had no limits to their authority were—
- Ⓕ guerrillas.
- Ⓖ prime ministers.
- Ⓗ dictators.
- Ⓙ prefects.

5 In 1952, which island adopted a constitution that made it a commonwealth of the United States?
- Ⓐ Dominican Republic
- Ⓑ St. Thomas
- Ⓒ Jamaica
- Ⓓ Puerto Rico

Use after reading Chapter 6, pages 192–217.

A Vast Land

Directions Gillian just returned from her vacation in South America. Below is a letter she wrote to a friend about some of the continent's special physical features. After Gillian mailed the letter, rain washed off some of the ink. To help Karla read the letter, fill in missing names.

January 23

Dear Karla:

    I had an amazing time in South America. I visited many cities. I also saw many beautiful landforms and bodies of water.

    The **1** ___________ Amazon ___________ River is part of the largest river system in the world. That was what I saw first. I did not have the chance to see the Río de la Plata, which consists of the

Paraná, Paraguay, and **2** ___________ Uruguay ___________ Rivers. I did learn that the Río de la Plata is not a river at all. It is an estuary, or the mouth of a river into which the ocean tide flows.

    Next I traveled to the **3** ___________ Guiana Highlands ___________. This area north of the Amazon River is mainly grasslands with scattered trees. Later I traveled south into the Andes Mountains. They stretch 4,500 miles from

4 ___________ Venezuela ___________ to the southern tip of South America. From the Andes I crossed the Central Plains to visit the Gran Chaco. This large region of scrub forests covers parts of Argentina, Paraguay, and

5 ___________ Bolivia ___________. I did not have the chance to see the other three areas of the Central Plains called the Llanos, the Selva, and

the **6** ___________ Pampas ___________.

    Before leaving South America, I went to the **7** ___________ Atacama ___________ Desert in northern Chile. It is one of the driest regions on Earth. Traveling south, I found myself in the part of South America closest to Antarctica. It's called

the **8** ___________ Tierra del Fuego ___________.

    I wish you could see this beautiful continent.

Your friend,

Gillian

(continued)

Name ______________________ Date ____________

Directions **While Gillian was in South America, she drew pictures of many different products that are produced there. But Gillian did not write down the countries in which she found them. Write the names of the products next to the countries where they are produced. Some can be matched with more than one country. Use your textbook to help you complete the activity.**

Argentina

airplanes
automobiles
bananas
beef

coffee
computers
grains

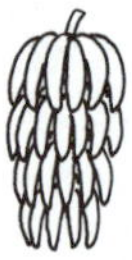

Bananas

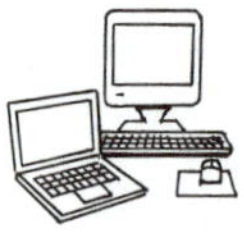

Computers

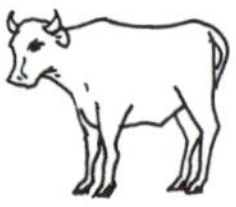

Beef

Brazil

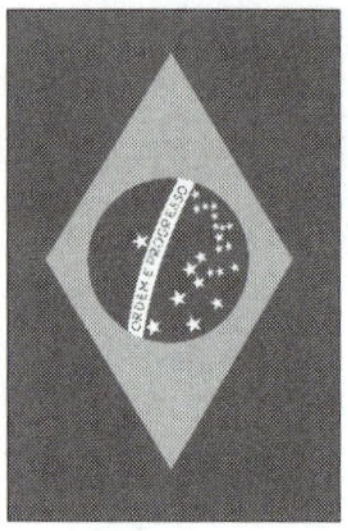

airplanes
automobiles
bananas
beef

coffee
computers
grains

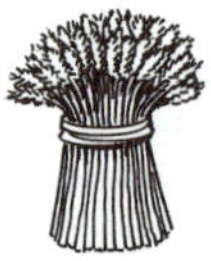

Grains

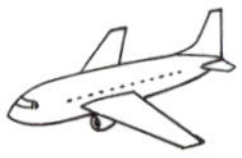

Airplanes

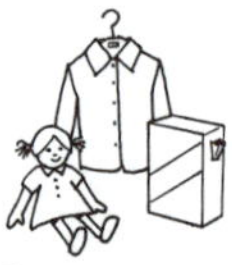

Consumer Goods

Venezuela

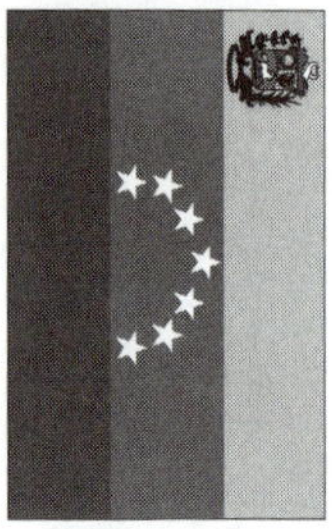

consumer goods

petroleum

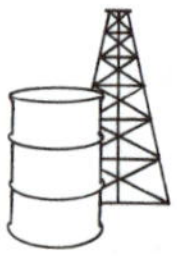

Petroleum

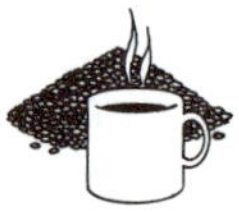

Coffee

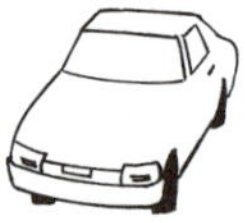

Automobiles

Chile

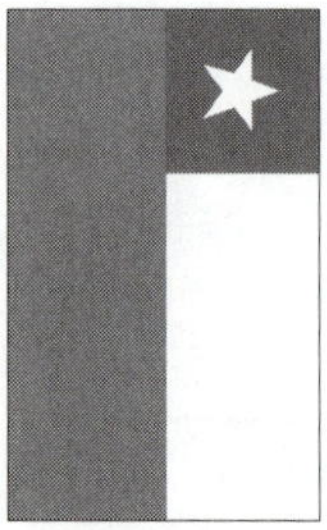

airplanes
automobiles

computers

Use after reading Chapter 7, Lesson 1, pages 220–227.

Name _______________________________________   Date _______________

Read a Map of Cultural Regions

Directions Cultural maps use symbols or colors to display information about the people living in a region. Use the cultural map of Brazil below to answer the questions on page 64.

Language Regions of Brazil

(continued)

Name ____ Date ____________________

Directions **Use the map of Brazil on page 63 to answer the following questions.**

1 What is the purpose of this map? to show the locations where different languages are spoken in the cities and states of Brazil

2 Which languages are spoken in Brazil? Portuguese and Native American languages

3 Which language is spoken in the city of São Paulo? Portuguese

4 Which language is spoken in most of Brazil's coastal regions?
Portuguese

5 Which languages are spoken in the Brazilian state of Acre?
Portuguese and Native American languages

6 Which state is farthest south and has citizens who speak both Portuguese and Native American languages? Paraná

7 Which language is spoken in most of Bahia? Portuguese

8 Which language is more widely spoken in the state of Roraima: Portuguese or a Native American language? Native American

9 In which of the following states are both Portuguese and Native American languages spoken: Sergipe, Mato Grosso, Rio Grande do Sul, or Pernambuco?
Mato Grosso

                    Use after reading Chapter 7, Skill Lesson, pages 228–229.

Cultures and Lifeways

Directions Explore the ruins of the Inca city of Machu Picchu. At the site, you will find several signs with information about the Incas and their empire. Each sign is missing important information. Complete each sign by writing short statements about the topic. Use your textbook to help you complete the activity.

Sample: Inca Government

The Incas were ruled by an emperor. The emperor forced the peoples

the Incas conquered to follow the Inca way of life.

Adapting to the Land

The Incas built terraces to make the land more suitable for farming.

The Incas built miles of roads to connect their empire.

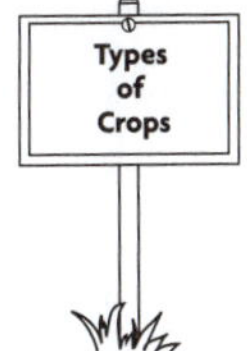

Types of Crops

The Incas grew beans, maize, squash, and potatoes.

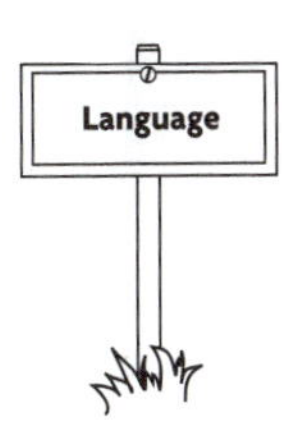

Language

The Inca native language is Quéchua. Later the Incas were required to

speak Spanish.

CHART AND GRAPH SKILLS
Read a Double-Bar Graph

Directions Double-bar graphs present two sets of statistics so that they can easily be compared. Study the graphs below, and use them to answer the questions on page 67.

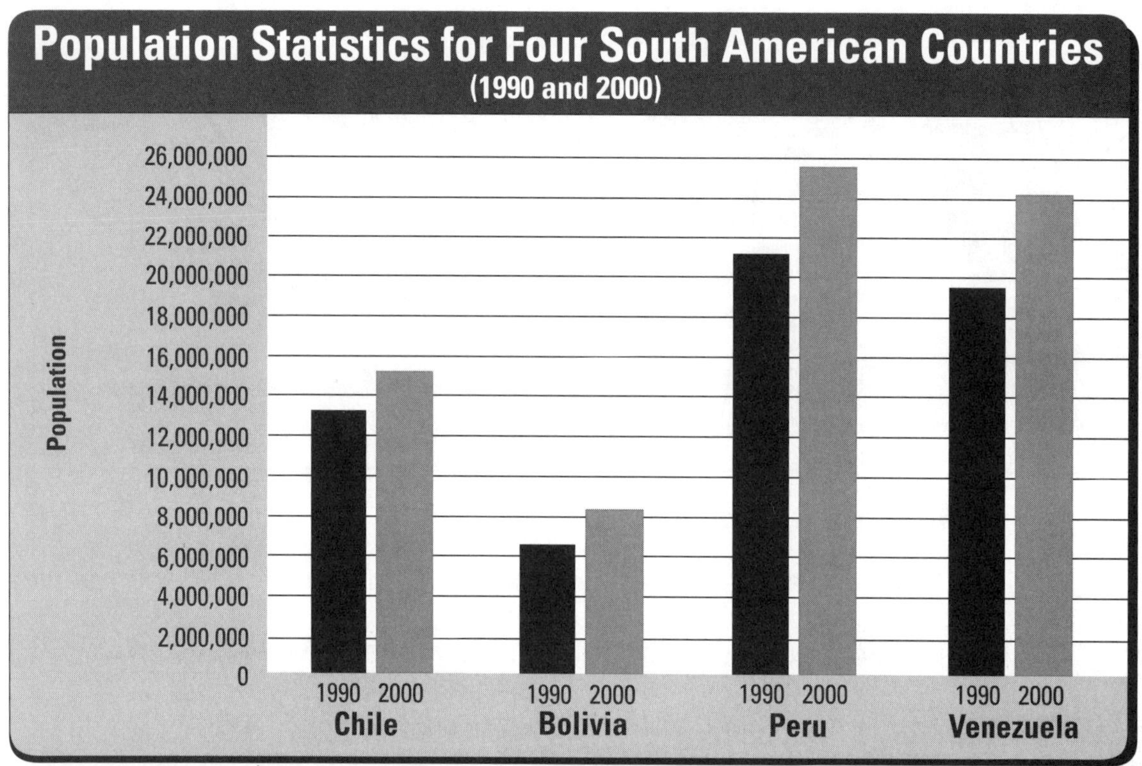

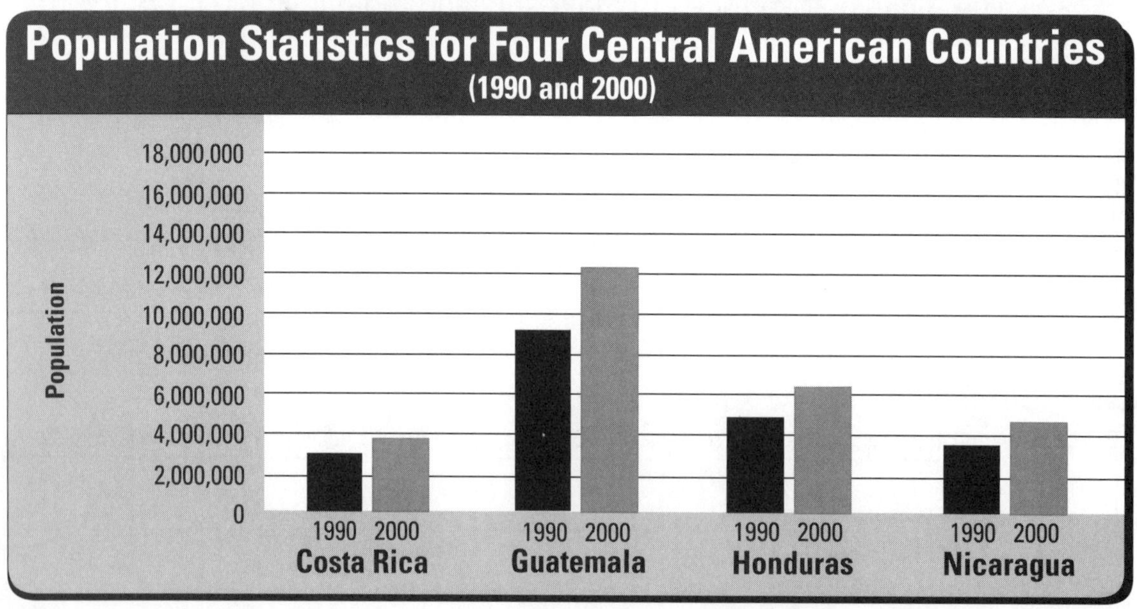

(continued)

          Use after reading Chapter 7, Skill Lesson, pages 238–239.

Name ____ Date ___________

1 What information is being compared in each of the double-bar graphs?

the populations of four countries in 1990 and 2000

2 Study the population statistics for Chile, Bolivia, Nicaragua, and Honduras. Which country had the largest population in both 1990 and 2000?

Chile

3 Study the population statistics for Bolivia, Nicaragua, and Honduras. Which country experienced the smallest population growth between 1990 and 2000?

Nicaragua

4 Do the graphs show that any country experienced a decline in population between 1990 and 2000? No

5 Which South American country had the largest population in both 1990 and 2000? Peru

6 Which Central American countries had smaller populations than Bolivia in both 1990 and 2000? Costa Rica, Honduras, and Nicaragua

7 List the South American and Central American countries that experienced a population growth of 3 or more million people between 1990 and 2000.

Peru, Venezuela, and Guatemala

8 Which South American and Central American countries experienced a population growth of about 2 million people between 1990 and 2000?

Bolivia, Chile, and Honduras

9 Which four countries had the largest populations in the year 2000? List them in order, largest to smallest. Peru, Venezuela, Chile, and Guatemala

10 Which country had the smallest population in both 1990 and 2000?

Costa Rica

Building a Future

Directions Simón Bolívar and José de San Martín were freedom fighters who played a major role in bringing independence to much of South America. Read the list of South American countries below. Sort the countries into those freed by Bolívar and those freed by San Martín. Then write each country's name next to the picture of the freedom fighter who helped that country gain its independence.

Argentina	Bolivia	Brazil	Chile	Colombia
Ecuador	Paraguay	Peru	Venezuela	

Simón Bolívar

Bolivia

Colombia

Ecuador

Peru

Venezuela

José de San Martín

Argentina

Chile

Peru

Directions Write a short paragraph to answer the following question. You may want to use your textbook to help you complete the activity.

Two South American countries listed above were not freed by Bolívar or San Martín. Name the countries, and describe how each gained its independence.

Paraguay and Brazil gained their independence without the help of Bolívar or San Martín. The Paraguayans declared their independence after overthrowing the Spanish viceroy in 1811. Brazil was able to gain its independence from Portugal without violence. The people of Brazil demanded their freedom, and the ruler of Brazil, Prince Pedro, granted it in 1822.

    Use after reading Chapter 7, Lesson 3, pages 240–243.

South America

Directions Complete these graphic organizers to show that, by combining what you read with what you already know, you can make inferences about cultural influences in South America.

DETAILS + KNOWLEDGE  **INFERENCE**

DETAILS	KNOWLEDGE	INFERENCE
The Incas settled in Peru and began conquering other civilizations. Spanish explorers who came to South America eventually conquered the Incas. Over the centuries many groups moved to South America, including Asians and Africans.	A region's culture is made up of the many different culture groups that have settled there.	The culture of South America is very diverse, combining the cultures of the native peoples and all of the groups who came to settle there later.

DETAILS	KNOWLEDGE	INFERENCE
South America has tall mountains, deserts, and hot, humid rain forests.	Few people live in mountainous and desert areas. Rivers are important for agriculture and transportation. Natural resources are valuable. People usually live in places where the temperatures are mild and cool.	Few people in South America live in the mountains, deserts, and rain forests. They live along rivers and where the climate is milder.

Name _______________________ Date _____________

Test Preparation

Directions Read each question and choose the best answer. Then fill in the circle for the answer you have chosen. Be sure to fill in the circle completely.

1 The _______ is one of the driest places on Earth.
- Ⓐ Gran Chaco
- **Ⓑ** Atacama Desert
- Ⓒ Patagonia
- Ⓓ Tierra del Fuego

2 The Amazon River is very important to trade in the area because—
- Ⓕ it carries one-fifth of Earth's fresh river water.
- Ⓖ it is a source of water for irrigation.
- Ⓗ it contains the largest amount of freshwater fish.
- **Ⓙ** it provides a transportation corridor.

3 Which group developed the first known civilization in South America?
- Ⓐ Incas
- **Ⓑ** Chavins
- Ⓒ Ges
- Ⓓ Mochicas

4 What percent of South America's population lives in urban areas?
- **Ⓕ** 70%
- Ⓖ 49%
- Ⓗ 80%
- Ⓙ 65%

5 A South American country that won its independence peacefully is—
- Ⓐ Bolivia.
- Ⓑ Peru.
- **Ⓒ** Brazil.
- Ⓓ Argentina.

Use after reading Chapter 7, pages 218–245.

Islands, Peninsulas, and Mountains

Directions Study the map below. Then use the map to help you answer the questions about Europe on page 72.

(continued)

Name ____ Date ___________________

Directions **Answer the questions below, using the map on page 71 and your textbook.**

1 Which three countries in Western Europe have more than one mountain range located in them? Italy, France, and Spain

2 Which Western European peninsula that lies to the north has only one country located on it? the Jutland Peninsula

3 Which Western European country is made up of more than one island?

the United Kingdom

4 Which two Western European countries have coasts on both the Mediterranean Sea and the Atlantic Ocean? Spain and France

5 In which two Western European countries can you find parts of the Alps and the Great European Plain? France and Germany

6 Which Western European countries are on the Iberian Peninsula?

Spain, Portugal, Andorra

7 Which Western European country is on the Balkan Peninsula?

Greece

8 Which river passes through the most Western European countries?

Rhine River

9 In which Western European country are the Sierra Nevada Mountains?

Spain

10 What is the name of the body of water that separates the United Kingdom from the European mainland? English Channel

     Use after reading Chapter 8, Lesson 1, pages 260–265.

MAP AND GLOBE SKILLS

Land Use and Products

Directions Study the products map of Germany below. Then answer the questions on page 74.

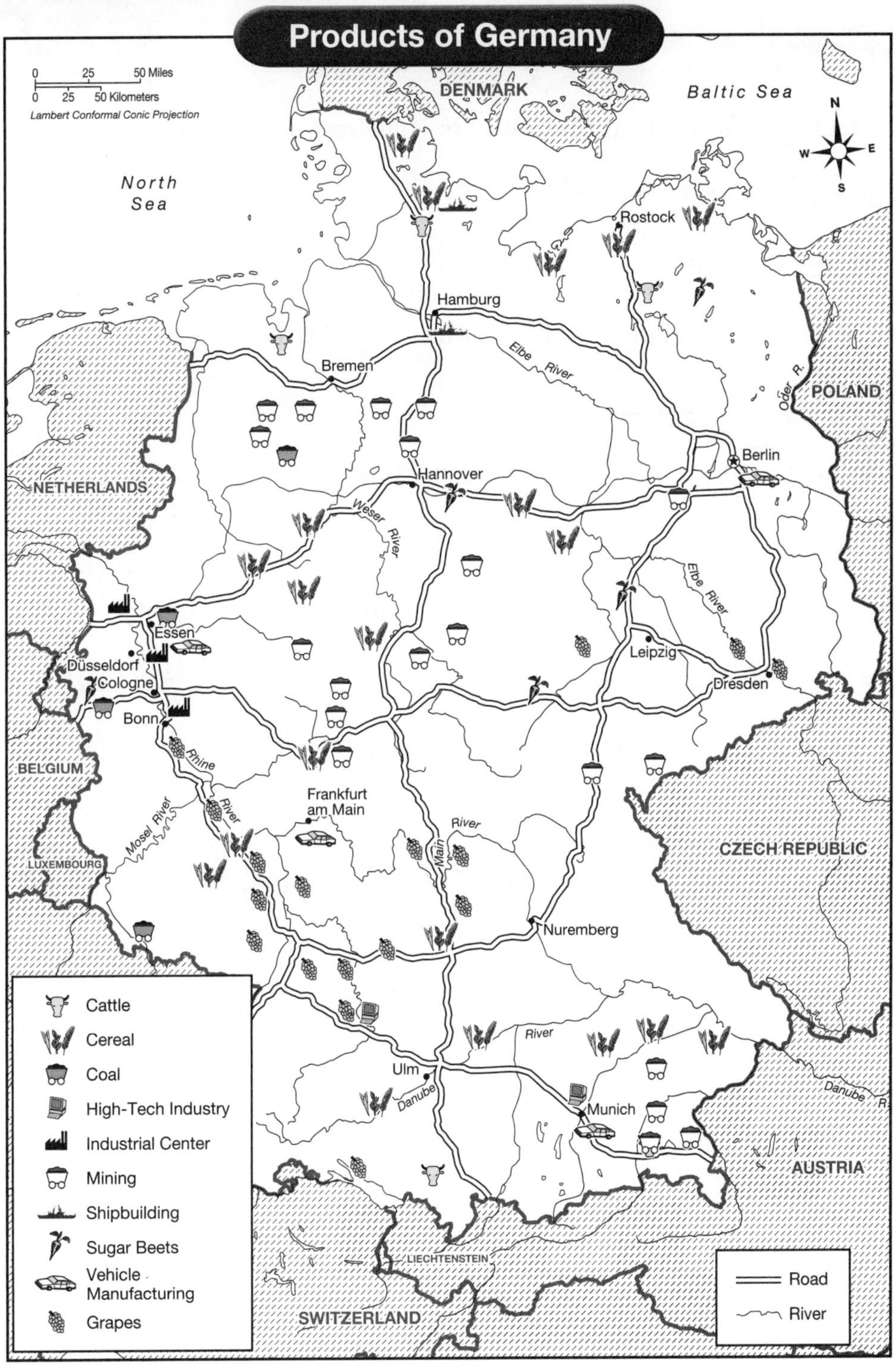

(continued)

Directions Use the map on page 73 to answer the questions below.

1 Which area of Germany has the most manufacturing and industry?

the area around the Rhine River, in the west

2 Circle Berlin, the capital of Germany. What are some of the area's products?

cars and coal

3 Recently, Germany's shipbuilding industry has been in decline. Which area of

Germany does this affect most? Northern Germany probably has been hurt the

most since most of the shipbuilding sites are near the coast.

4 In which region of Germany are most of its grapes grown?

the southwest

5 What product is found in the areas of both Essen and Bremen?

coal

6 If you traveled from Rostock to Berlin, what kinds of crops might you see in fields

along the way? cereals

7 On the map, draw a travel route from one city in Germany to another. Then list
three different kinds of products that you would pass along the way.

Starting City	Product #1	Product #2	Product #3	Ending City
Answers will vary.				

Western Europe Through the Ages

Directions Match the events from Western European history listed in Box A with the effects that they helped cause listed in Box B. Write the letter of each effect in the space provided. Use your textbook to help you complete the activity.

Box A

Cause

_**g**_ **1** Alexander the Great builds a huge empire.

_**b**_ **2** The Roman Empire conquers much of Europe.

_**h**_ **3** The Roman Empire falls.

_**c**_ **4** Johannes Gutenberg invents a new way to print books.

_**f**_ **5** Mercantilism becomes the new economic system.

_**e**_ **6** Advances in science introduce new ways of manufacturing.

_**a**_ **7** Countries compete for wealth and colonies.

_**d**_ **8** World War I destroys much of Western Europe.

Box B

Effect

a. People develop strong feelings of nationalism.

b. Latin becomes the basis for many languages now spoken in Europe.

c. Information begins to spread more quickly.

d. Dictators come to power in several European nations.

e. People begin to move from farms to cities.

f. Western European nations set up colonies around the world.

g. Greek culture is spread.

h. Art, education, industry, and trade are nearly forgotten.

Directions Review the events above. Then choose one event and explain the cause and its effect in detail.

Answers will vary, but should present sufficient detail about the cause and effect.

____

____

____

____

Use after reading Chapter 8, Lesson 2, pages 268–273.   **Activity Book ▪ 75**

Culture Unites and Culture Divides

Directions Read the passages below about Western European culture. Then read the statements that follow them. Decide whether each statement is a fact or an opinion, and explain your choice.

1 Many languages are spoken in Western Europe. Some countries, such as Switzerland, have several official languages. Others, such as France, have only one. In the United Kingdom, people speak English, but with different accents. Many people in Western Europe also speak some English.

FACT or OPINION: English is the best language for people to speak.

Opinion. Although English is spoken by many people, that does not mean English is better than other languages.

2 Although most people in Western Europe are Roman Catholic, other religions are also practiced in the region. Some people practice Protestantism, a group of Christian denominations that split away from the Roman Catholic Church 500 years ago. Protestants and Catholics fought long wars against each other. Although people are tolerant of different religions in most parts of Western Europe, there is still some conflict. Today Catholics and Protestants continue to fight in Northern Ireland.

FACT or OPINION: Religious differences can lead to violence.

Fact. The wars between Protestants and Catholics were the result of religious differences.

3 For hundreds of years, people have moved to Western Europe's cities in search of work. In the last century, many people have arrived from places such as Africa, Asia, Australia, and the Caribbean. In some countries migration has resulted in conflict. In other places, people from different ethnic groups have gotten along peacefully.

FACT or OPINION: Western Europe is very diverse culturally.

Fact. People from all over the world have settled in Western Europe.

Unity in Europe

Directions The European Union is an important economic unit. It was originally formed in the 1950s as the European Coal and Steel Community and later became known as the European Community. Fill in the names of the countries that joined each form of the organization. Then read the statements that follow. Write the name of the country described by each statement. You may want to use your textbook or the Internet to help you complete the activity.

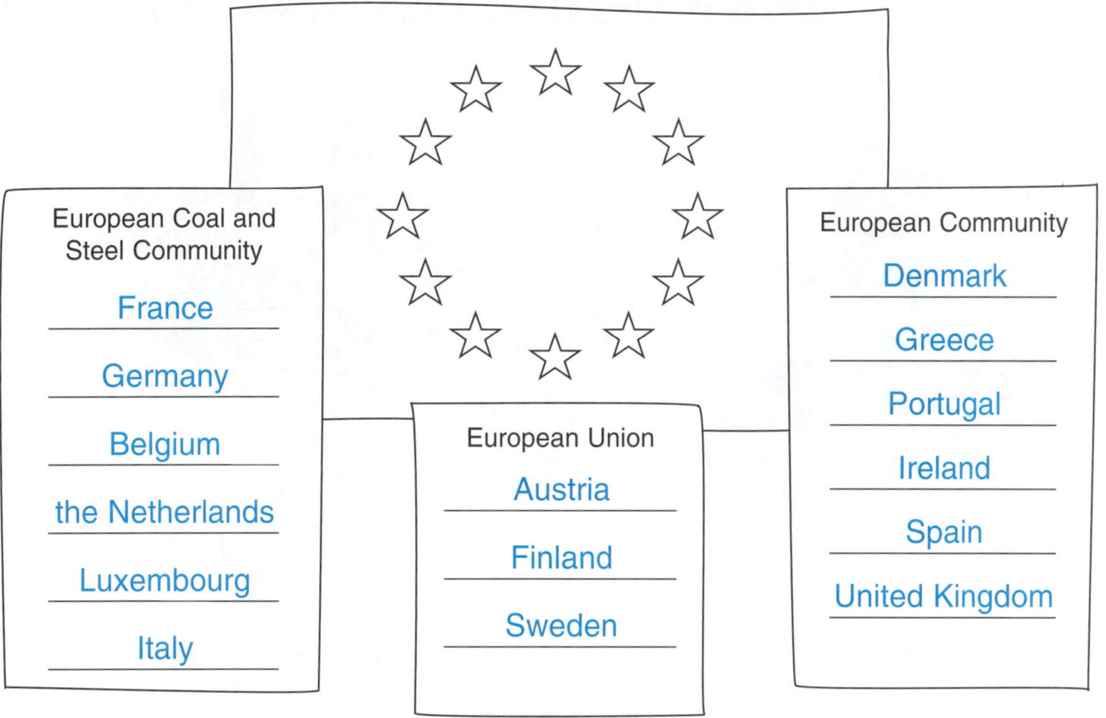

1 This large republic, home to the *Train Grande Vitesse*, was one of the original members of the European Union. France

2 This country is not a member of the European Union, although EU members surround it. Switzerland

3 This northern country is famous for its shipyards and was one of the last to join the European Union. Finland

4 This tiny country was one of the original countries in the European Union. It is also famous for banking and finance. Luxembourg

5 This island country, which joined the European Union later on, was the first in which the rights of its citizens were protected. United Kingdom

READING SKILLS

Read an Editorial Cartoon

Directions Examine the editorial cartoon below. Then answer the questions that follow it.

1 According to the sign, what does the mountain symbolize?

a stable European economy

2 What is the occupation of the two people on the mountain? Explain your answer.

They probably work in business or politics, since they are wearing suits and

carrying briefcases.

3 What is the topic of this editorial cartoon? The topic is whether the economy is

getting better or worse.

4 What do the two people think about the economy? They think that the economy is

going to get better.

5 What do you think the cartoonist thinks about this topic?

The cartoonist thinks that the economy is about to get much worse.

Western Europe

Directions **Complete this graphic organizer to show that you understand cause-and-effect relationships in Western Europe.**

| CAUSE | → | EFFECT |

Winds blow over the warm water in the North Atlantic Drift and across Western Europe.

→ **Much of northwestern Europe has a mild climate.**

Gutenberg invented movable type.

→ Books became available to more people.

Europeans encountered Muslim states.

→ **Europeans and Muslims began to exchange knowledge and ideas.**

Religious and political differences exist between Catholics and Protestants in Northern Ireland.

→ Acts of violence and terror occur.

Many Western European nations are working together to improve their economies.

→ **Many Western European nations have strong economies.**

Name _______________________________   Date ___________

Test Preparation

Directions Read each question and choose the best answer. Then fill in the circle for the answer you have chosen. Be sure to fill in the circle completely.

1 Which of the following is NOT a major land region in the mainland of Western Europe?
- Ⓐ the Great European Plain
- Ⓑ the Central Uplands
- Ⓒ the Alpine Mountain System
- Ⓓ the Ruhr Valley

2 _______ was an economic system in which a nation's exports had to be greater than its imports.
- Ⓕ Manorialism
- Ⓖ Mercantilism
- Ⓗ Socialism
- Ⓙ Industrialism

3 The Western European country with three official languages is—
- Ⓐ Spain.
- Ⓑ Norway.
- Ⓒ Switzerland.
- Ⓓ Germany.

4 Many cities in Western Europe have been influenced by other cultures. In Cordoba, Spain, the _______ shows the influence of the Muslims who ruled parts of Spain.
- Ⓕ food
- Ⓖ theater
- Ⓗ architecture
- Ⓙ music

5 A major industry in France is—
- Ⓐ agriculture.
- Ⓑ natural gas.
- Ⓒ coal.
- Ⓓ iron ore.

     Use after reading Chapter 8, pages 258–291.

Varied Lands and Varied Resources

Directions Study the chart below. It shows some of the countries of Eastern Europe, their special physical features, and their products. Use the chart to answer the questions on page 82.

Country	Physical Features	Products	
Czech Republic	Bohemian Forest Sudety Mountains	cement iron machinery plastic	pottery steel textiles wood
Estonia	low coastal plain thick forest 1,400 lakes 800 islands	farm products fish forest products oil shale	
Hungary	Danube River Tisza River thermal springs many lakes	fruits peppers vegetables	
Lithuania	low coastal plain thick forest	amber farm products fish forest products	
Macedonia	Balkan Mountains	cotton fruit rice	
Moldova	Dniester River Pruth River	tractors clothing corn	various consumer goods grapes
Poland	Vistula River Carpathian Mountains	automobiles machinery steel	
Romania	Carpathian Mountains Transylvanian Alps Danube River	farm products gold lignite silver	
Slovenia	Limestone caverns	forest products variety of crops	

(continued)

Name ____ Date _________________

1 How are the products of Lithuania and Estonia different?

Lithuania has amber, and Estonia has oil shale.

2 What physical feature do Poland and Romania have in common?

the Carpathian Mountains

3 Which country on the chart has the widest variety of products?

the Czech Republic

4 Which two countries on the chart do not have products grown on farms?

Poland and the Czech Republic

5 Which two countries on the chart rely on farming for all their major products?

Hungary and Macedonia

Directions Use the chart and your textbook to write a descriptive paragraph that compares two countries of Eastern Europe. Be sure to include the countries' physical features and products.

Students' responses will vary but should include details that compare the

countries' landforms, bodies of water, resources, and products.

Name ______________________ Date ______________

Centuries of Change

Directions **The Eastern European countries were invaded many times and were ruled by many different conquerors. Using the information in your textbook, write the names of the invaders and rulers from the list below next to their descriptions in the chart. Some names may be used more than once, and others may not be used at all.**

Invaders and Rulers

Huns	Poland
Russia	Austria-Hungary
Magyars	Byzantine Empire
Ottoman Empire	Soviet Union
Visigoths	Slavs

1 These people moved through the Carpathian Mountains and settled in what is now Hungary.	Magyars
2 This empire controlled the southern region of Eastern Europe by 1680.	Ottoman Empire
3 This country divided up Poland with Austria and Prussia, taking all the eastern areas of Poland.	Russia
4 This country took control of Bosnia and Herzegovina in 1908.	Austria-Hungary
5 This empire lost Hungary to Austria in the 1700s.	Ottoman Empire
6 This country set up communist-style governments in many countries after World War II.	Soviet Union
7 This country was divided up into many smaller countries after World War I.	Austria-Hungary
8 This migrating people from Asia traveled to Eastern Europe.	Huns
9 This empire lasted almost 1,000 years after splitting from the Western Roman Empire.	Byzantine Empire
10 These people settled what is now Poland, the Czech Republic, Slovakia, and the western Balkan countries.	Slavs

Use after reading Chapter 9, Lesson 2, pages 300–305.

MAP AND GLOBE SKILLS
Identify Changing Borders

(continued)

Name ____ Date _______________________

Directions By comparing maps from different time periods, you can learn how
the borders of countries have changed over time. Look at the maps on page 84
that show how Poland was divided at different times. Then answer the questions
below.

1 Which countries increased their land area in 1772? Prussia, Austria, and Russia

____

2 Which country's borders did not change between 1793 and 1795?

the Ottoman Empire

3 Which country lost territory in 1772, 1793, and 1795? Poland

4 Which country added the largest amount of land to its territory between 1763 and 1795?

Russia

5 Name the Polish cities that Prussia gained in 1772, 1793, and 1795.

Danzig, Posen, and Warsaw

6 How did Prussia's borders change in 1772? Prussia grew and was able to connect

its two separate parts.

7 Which countries did Russia border in 1772? Poland and the Ottoman Empire

____

8 The Polish cities listed below fell under foreign control during each of Poland's
divisions. Sort the names of the cities by the year they fell under foreign control.
Write each city's name in the correct column.

Danzig	Lemberg	Cracow	Minsk	Warsaw

1772	1793	1795
Danzig	Minsk	Cracow
Lemberg		Warsaw

Times of Freedom

Directions Eastern Europe has undergone many changes since the fall of communism. Use the graphic organizer below to describe Eastern Europe after communist rule. Write three details to support each main idea.

Eastern Europe After Communism

The End of Communism

Trouble between ethnic groups has been a problem in Yugoslavia since the fall of communism. Possible answers: 1. Croatia and Serbia fought a war because Serbs living in Croatia did not want to live under the control of the Croats. 2. Serbs, Croats, and Muslims fought a war to control Bosnia and Herzegovina. Serbian president Slobodan Milosevic encouraged ethnic cleansing of other ethnic groups. 3. People in Kosovo with Albanian ancestors rebelled, trying to create an independent state. Serbian president Slobodan Milosevic sent in forces to stop the rebellion, killing many people.

Forming New Governments

Many nations in Eastern Europe chose to set up democratic governments, but they had different forms. Possible answers: 1. Several countries, including the Czech Republic, Slovakia, and Hungary, became parliamentary democracies. 2. Poland, Romania, Yugoslavia, and Moldova became republics. 3. Bosnia and Herzegovina formed a unique government in which three different presidents are elected and share power.

Changing Economies

People in Eastern Europe faced many difficulties as the industries in their countries were privatized. Possible answers: 1. People could not afford to buy the privatized factories, so many of them closed. 2. Many people lost their jobs when the factories closed. 3. The price of goods went up, making it difficult for many to buy basic products.

Use after reading Chapter 9, Lesson 3, pages 308–313.

Varied Cultures

Directions Read each of the clues below. Use the clues to complete the crossword puzzle.

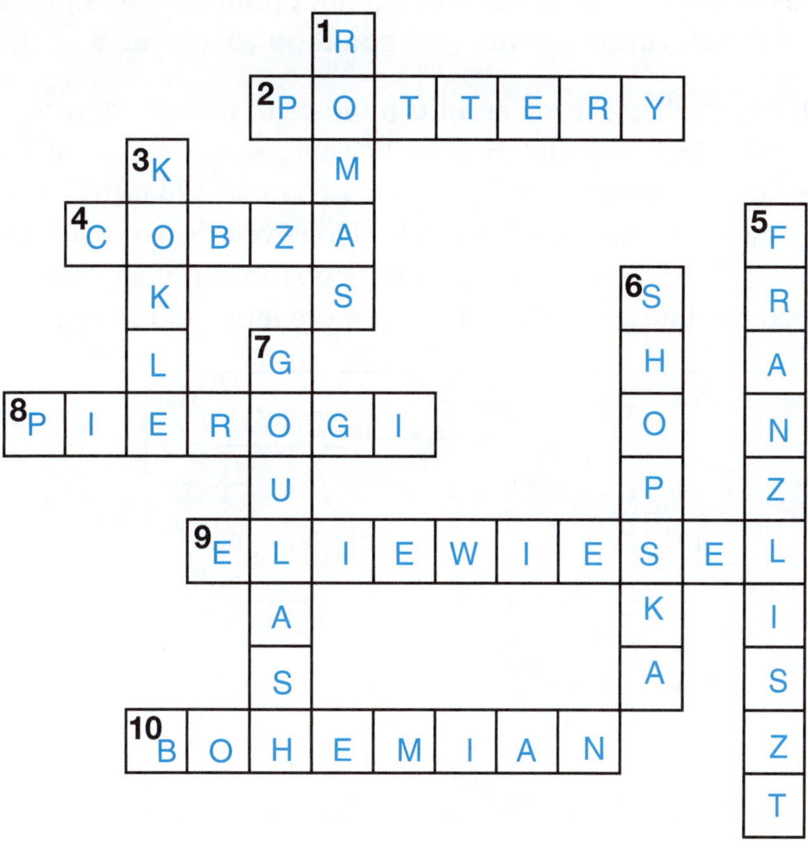

Across

2 Traditional Slovenian _______ is both beautiful and useful.

4 The _______ is a musical instrument in Moldova.

8 At dinner in Poland, you might be served a _______.

9 _______ wrote *Night*, a book about his experiences during the Holocaust. (two words)

10 _______ glass, made in the Czech Republic, is some of the best in the world.

Down

1 The _______ are a people who do not have a country of their own.

3 A traditional stringed instrument of Latvia is the _______.

5 The Hungarian composer _______ wrote many famous pieces of classical music. (two words)

6 A traditional salad eaten in Bulgaria is _______.

7 Many Hungarians eat _______, a spicy stew with many ingredients.

CITIZENSHIP SKILLS
Resolve Conflicts

Directions **Read the description of a fictional conflict below. Then number the steps to show the order in which the conflict could be resolved.**

Residents of a small town called Presno and the builders of its new airport are in conflict. Trucks carrying building materials to the construction site are driving very fast down Presno's main street. The residents of Presno are worried that their children may be hurt or killed by one of the fast-moving trucks. However, the construction crews need to get supplies to the construction site as quickly as possible. If they do not, the airport will not be finished on time and will cost much more money to complete.

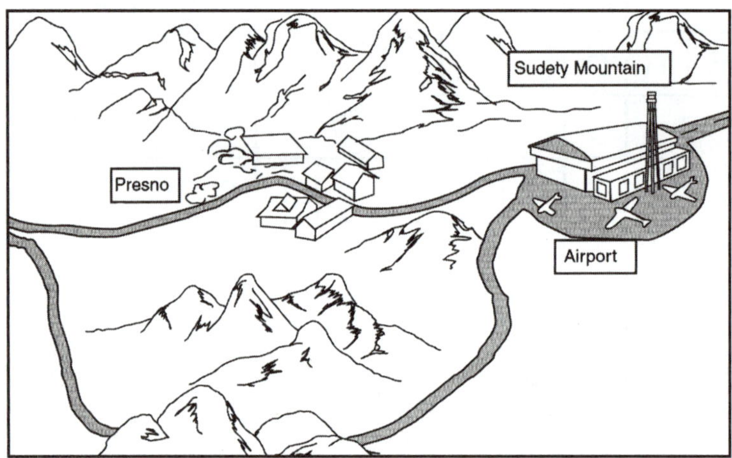

Step ___4___ The residents of Presno offer a compromise that during school hours, when children are indoors, the builders can send trucks through Presno to get to the airport more quickly. The remainder of the time, the trucks will go around Presno. The builders accept the compromise.

Step ___3___ The builders say that they will send their trucks through Presno more slowly but that they must use the most direct road possible. The residents say that is still too dangerous. They ask the builders to send some of their trucks around Presno.

Step ___1___ Both sides agree that they want the airport to be finished on time without anybody being hurt.

Step ___5___ Residents of Presno watch the trucks to make sure that they only drive through town during the scheduled hours. If they see a truck going through town when it should be driving around it, they report it to the builders and the police.

Step ___2___ The residents and the skuilders of the airport meet to discuss the issue. The residents ask the builders to send their trucks around Presno rather than through it. The builders believe that would take too long and slow down construction. Both groups go back and discuss what they can give up in order to reach an agreement.

Eastern Europe

Directions Complete this graphic organizer to show that you understand how to determine points of view about fighting in Kosovo.

SPEAKER	REASON FOR MAKING STATEMENT	POINT OF VIEW	WORDS THAT SIGNAL POINT OF VIEW
Bill Clinton, President of the United States	**NATO's involvement in the bombings in Serbia**	He believes that ethnic cleansing is bad and should be punished if we are to prevent it in the future.	all we would do
Doug Hostetter, International Secretary of the Fellowship of Reconciliation	**NATO's involvement in the bombings in Serbia**	He believes war is bad and that it is better to talk through problems than to use force.	I can only think

Name _______________________ Date _______________

Test Preparation

Directions Read each question and choose the best answer. Then fill in the circle for the answer you have chosen. Be sure to fill in the circle completely.

1 A natural feature that attracts visitors to the Czech Republic is the—
- Ⓐ Danube River.
- Ⓑ Carpathian Mountain Range.
- Ⓒ Thermal Spring.
- Ⓓ Bohemian Forest.

2 Which empire lasted almost 1,000 years by developing a strong government and economy?
- Ⓕ Ottoman
- Ⓖ Byzantine
- Ⓗ Roman
- Ⓙ Austrian

3 What happened at the end of World War I?
- Ⓐ The Ottoman Empire was created.
- Ⓑ New countries were formed in Eastern Europe.
- Ⓒ Austria-Hungary was united into one country.
- Ⓓ The Central Powers gained control of most of Eastern Europe.

4 Once new democracies were in place, the new privatized industries—
- Ⓕ were run by the governments.
- Ⓖ caused unemployment and inflation.
- Ⓗ flourished without government control.
- Ⓙ did not allow outside countries to bring in new business.

5 Paczki, shopska, and pierogi are all kinds of—
- Ⓐ traditional food.
- Ⓑ opera.
- Ⓒ rugs.
- Ⓓ stringed instruments.

Use after reading Chapter 9, pages 292–323.

Landforms and Climates

Directions Use the map and clues below to help you unscramble the names of the countries and landforms in the Commonwealth of Independent States. Write the unscrambled words in the space provided.

1. the site of the Chernobyl disaster of 1986

   _________ Ukraine _________
   EANKURI

2. the "land of fire," where oil and natural gas are located

   _________ Azerbaijan _________
   ENIBZAAJRA

3. the barrier between Europe and Asia

   _________ Ural Mountains _________
   LAUR SNUTONMIA

4. the largest country in the world, stretching through Europe and Asia

   _________ Russia _________
   SIRASU

5. the country located in the Caucasus Mountains that has inactive volcanoes

   _________ Armenia _________
   RANAIME

6. a country with many forests and rivers that provide its electricity

   _________ Belarus _________
   USLAREB

7. the divider between the Caucasus Mountains and the desert countries

   _________ Caspian Sea _________
   IPNACSA EAS

Use after reading Chapter 10, Lesson 1, pages 326–331.

CHART AND GRAPH SKILLS
Read a Climograph

Directions Using the information in the tables below, complete the climographs for the capitals of Ukraine and Azerbaijan. You may want to use your textbook to help you complete the activity. Then answer the questions on page 93.

Kiev, Ukraine

	JAN	FEB	MAR	APR	MAY	JUNE	JULY	AUG	SEP	OCT	NOV	DEC
Temperature (°F)	22°	24°	33°	48°	59°	65°	67°	66°	57°	47°	36°	28°
Precipitation (in.)	1.90	1.80	1.50	1.90	2.10	2.90	3.50	2.70	1.90	1.40	2.00	2.10

Baku, Azerbaijan

	JAN	FEB	MAR	APR	MAY	JUNE	JULY	AUG	SEP	OCT	NOV	DEC
Temperature (°F)	38°	38°	42°	53°	62°	69°	75°	75°	68°	58°	50°	42°
Precipitation (in.)	0.90	0.90	1.00	0.70	0.60	0.20	0.10	0.30	0.70	1.10	1.40	1.10

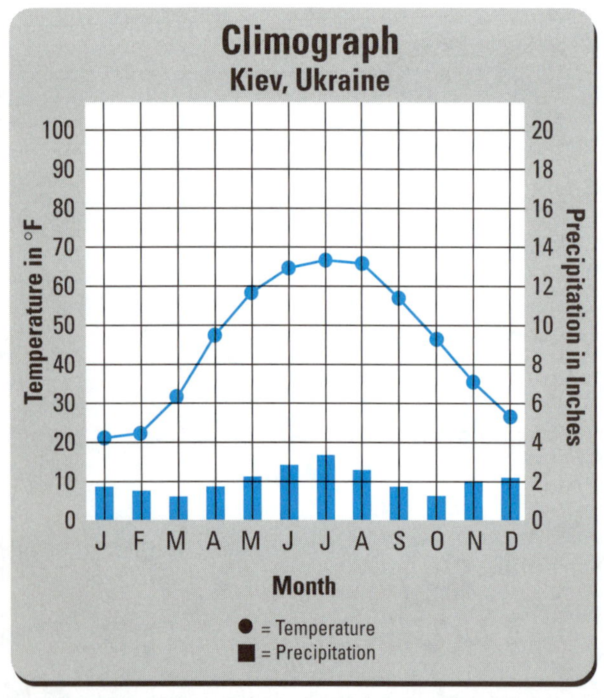

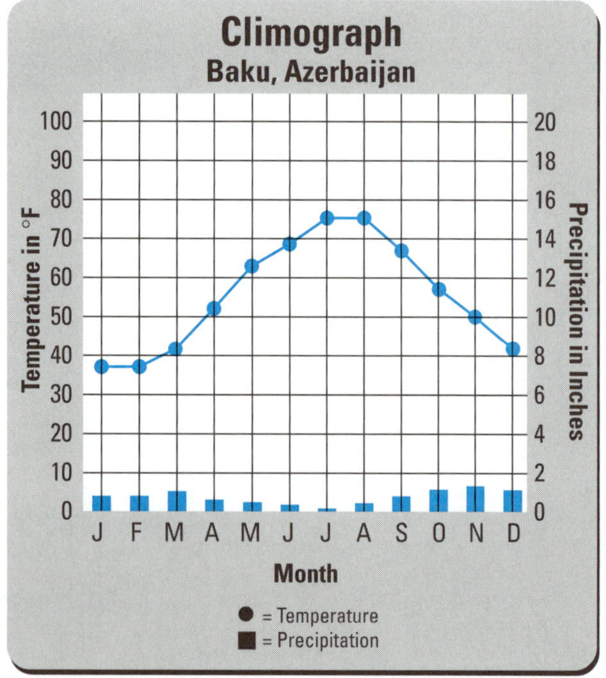

(continued)

Name ____   Date _______________________

1 Which city has a winter with more precipitation? Kiev

2 Which city has a warmer winter? Baku

3 During which months is Baku the hottest? July and August

4 During which season does Baku get the most rain? During which season does it get the least rain? autumn; summer

5 Cotton grows best in warmer areas where the temperature does not usually drop below freezing. If you were going to plant cotton near one of these cities, which of the two cities would you choose? Explain your answer. Baku; The cotton should be planted near Baku because it has much higher temperatures than Kiev. The average temperature in Baku is never below freezing.

6 Corn grows best in areas that receive 18 to 25 inches of rain a year. If you were going to plant corn near one of these cities, which of the two cities would you choose? Explain your answer. Kiev; The corn should be planted near Kiev, which gets twenty-five inches of rain a year. Baku gets less than ten inches of rain a year, and corn would not grow well there.

7 If farmers usually plant corn when the temperature of the soil reaches 55° Fahrenheit, during which month might you plant corn near the city you chose in number six? Explain your answer. In May, when the average temperature reaches almost 60° in Ukraine.

The Soviet Union Rises and Falls

Directions Study the time line of Russian history. Use the time line to answer the questions.

1 How long after the Russian Revolution began did Lenin and the Bolsheviks form the Soviet Union? five years

2 Who was the last czar of Russia?

Nicholas II

3 How long did the Soviet Union last?

sixty-nine years

4 How long was Mikhail Gorbachev the leader of the Soviet Union? six years

5 Who was elected the leader of Russia in 2000?

Vladimir Putin

Directions Write a paragraph describing the events of the Russian Revolution and the founding of the Soviet Union. Use the information in the time line and your textbook.

Students' answers will vary but should include descriptions of the following:

the Russian Revolution of 1917, the abdication and death of Nicholas II, and the

forming of the Soviet Union in 1922.

MAP AND GLOBE SKILLS

Read a Time Zone Map

Directions The Commonwealth of Independent States includes many different time zones. Study the time zone map below. Then complete the activities on page 96.

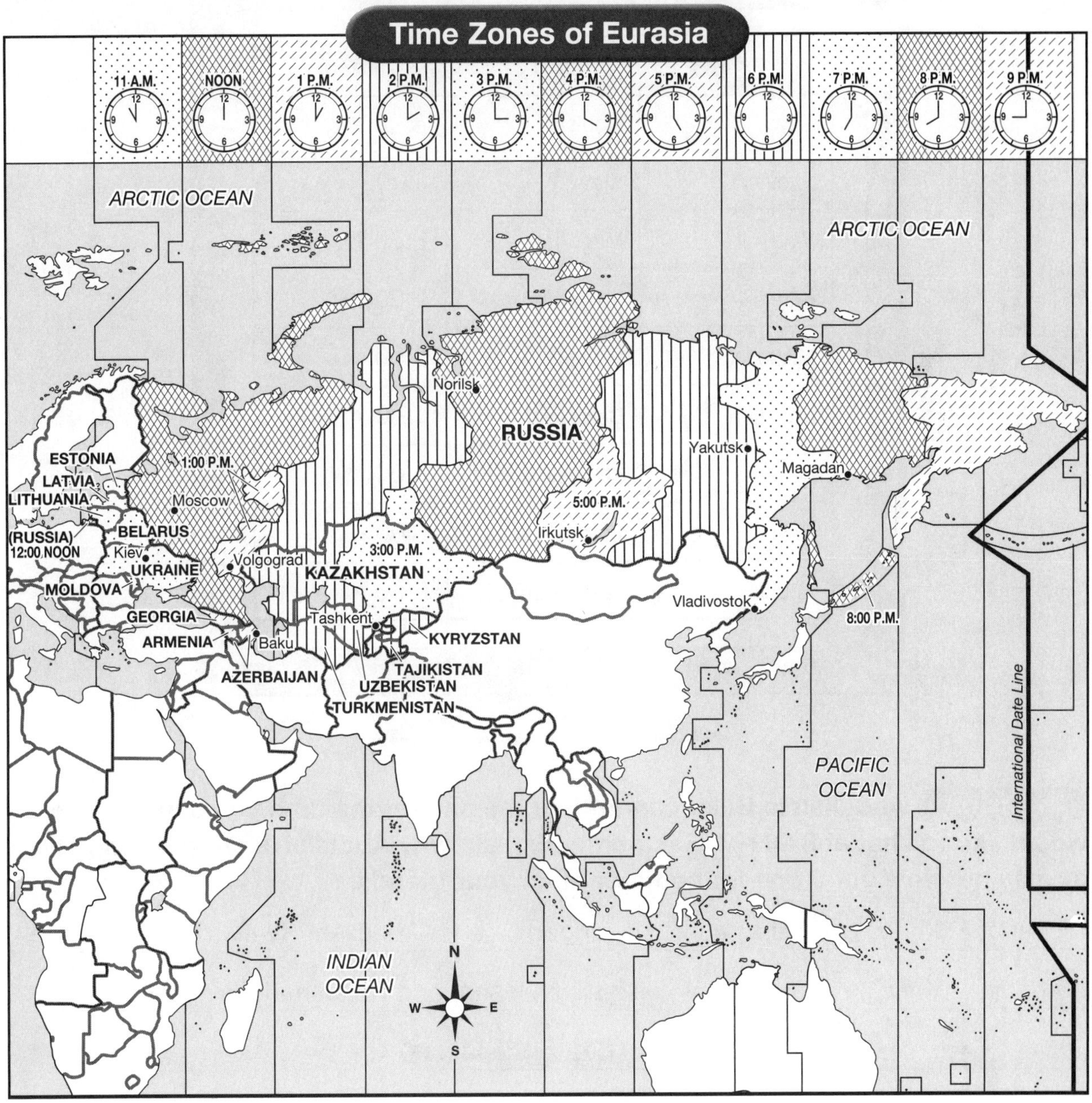

Time Zones of Eurasia

(continued)

Directions Imagine that you live in Moscow and want to schedule an online chat with your friends in cities across the CIS. The time differences between the cities make communicating with your friends difficult. Use the time zone map on page 95 to help you fill in the local time each of your friends would need to join a chat with you at noon Moscow time.

Friend	City	Time
Anya	Norilsk	4:00 P.M.
Svetlana	Kiev	11:00 A.M.
Vladimir	Magadan	8:00 P.M.
Katerina	Volgograd	1:00 P.M.
Mikhail	Irkutsk	5:00 P.M.
Abdullah	Baku	12:00 P.M.
Natasha	Yakutsk	6:00 P.M.
Raisa	Vladivostok	6:00 P.M.
Sophia	Tashkent	2:00 P.M.

Directions Abdullah in Baku cannot join the chat at the time you suggest. He would like to chat at 8:00 P.M. Baku time. Explain why Abdullah's suggestion may or may not be a good one for some or all of your friends.

A chat at 8:00 P.M. Baku time would be a good time for Abdullah, Svetlana, Sophia, and Katerina. However, Anya, Vladimir, Mikhail, Natasha, and Raisa may have difficulty joining. Their local times fall between 11:00 P.M. and 3:00 A.M.

   Use after reading Chapter 10, Skill Lesson, pages 340–341.

Times of Change

Directions Many aspects of life in the Commonwealth of Independent States (CIS) have changed since the fall of the Soviet Union. Use the information in your textbook to complete the tables below. In some places you will have to write about what life was like under the Soviet Union. In other places you will have to write about what life was like after the Soviet Union.

Under the Soviet Union . . .	After the Soviet Union . . .
1 Large sports arenas were built.	Most large sports arenas are closed.
2 People were not allowed to practice religion openly.	People begin to practice religion openly.
3 The government owned many factories, farms, shops, and other businesses.	Many businesses are sold to private owners and private companies.
4 People were guaranteed jobs, but they could not choose the jobs they wanted.	People get to choose their jobs, but many more are unemployed.
5 The space program was failing because there was not enough money.	Russian cosmonauts work aboard the International Space Station.
6 There were no wealthy social classes.	A new social class of wealthy citizens appears.

Directions Choose another aspect of life in the CIS, such as culture, language, food, athletics, or city life. Explain how that aspect of life has or has not changed since the fall of the Soviet Union.

Students' answers will vary.

____

____

____

Russia and the Eurasian Republics

Directions Complete this graphic organizer to show that you understand how to categorize different landforms in Russia.

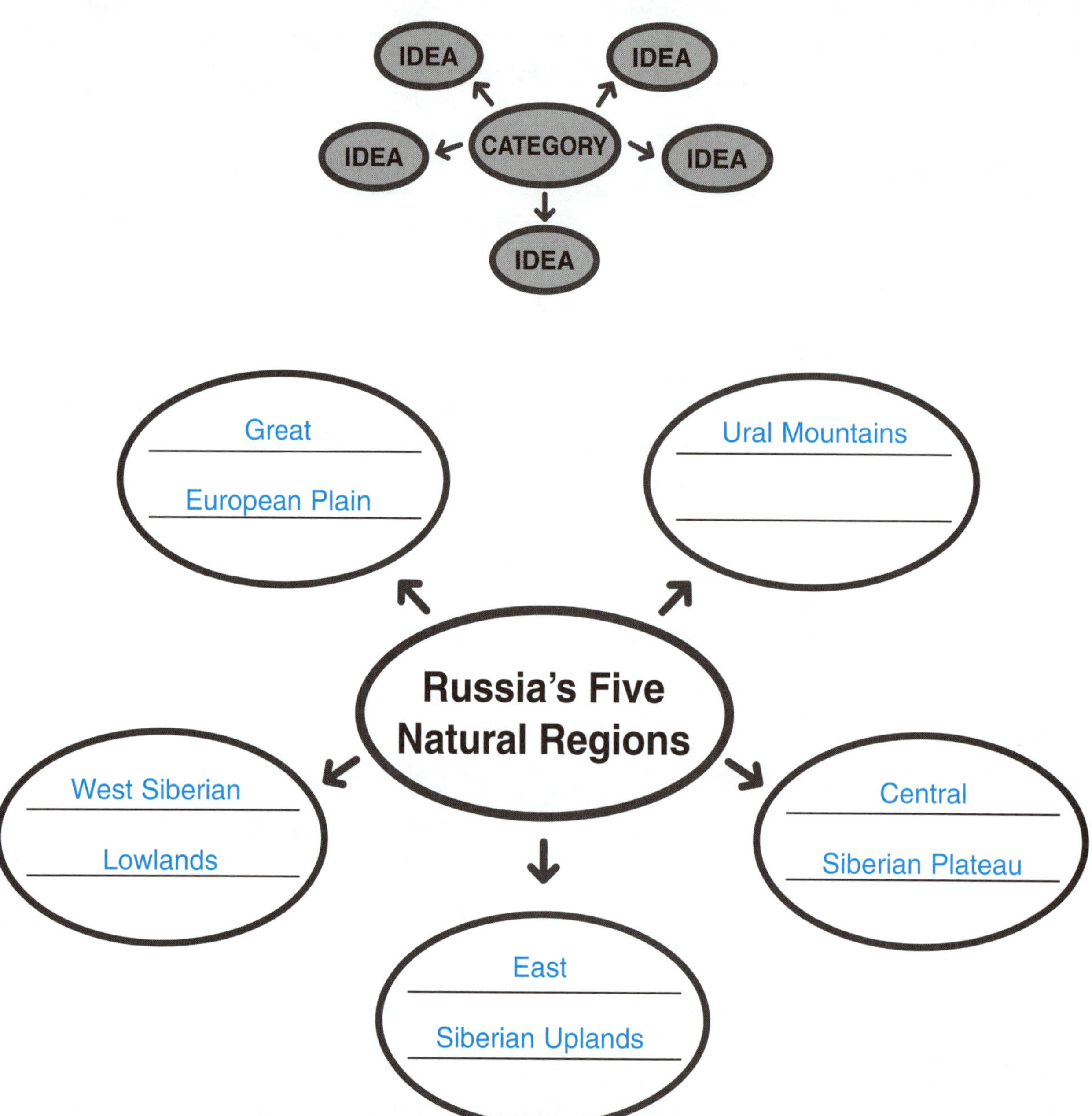

Name _______________________ Date _______________

Test Preparation

Directions **Read each question and choose the best answer. Then fill in the circle for the answer you have chosen. Be sure to fill in the circle completely.**

1 What forms a natural barrier between Europe and Asia?
- Ⓐ the Volga River
- **Ⓑ** the Ural Mountains
- Ⓒ the Siberian Lowlands
- Ⓓ the Northern European Plains

2 _______ covers 233,000 square miles and is about the size of Texas.
- Ⓕ Kazakhstan
- Ⓖ Belarus
- Ⓗ Russia
- **Ⓙ** Ukraine

3 What brought an end to the rule of the czars in Russia?
- **Ⓐ** the Russian Revolution and the establishment of communism
- Ⓑ the death of Catherine the Great
- Ⓒ the rule of the dictator Stalin
- Ⓓ World War II

4 Boris Yeltsin became Russia's first democratic leader in—
- Ⓕ 1985.
- Ⓖ 1989.
- Ⓗ 1993.
- **Ⓙ** 1991.

5 Before the fall of the Soviet Union, citizens in the Commonwealth of Independent States were not allowed to—
- Ⓐ play chess.
- Ⓑ tell folktales.
- **Ⓒ** practice religion.
- Ⓓ eat traditional foods.

Use after reading Chapter 10, pages 324–349.

Land of Contrasts

Directions Study the map of Southwest Asia. Then read the sentences that follow. Provide supporting details for each sentence, using information from the map and your textbook. Use a separate sheet of paper, if necessary.

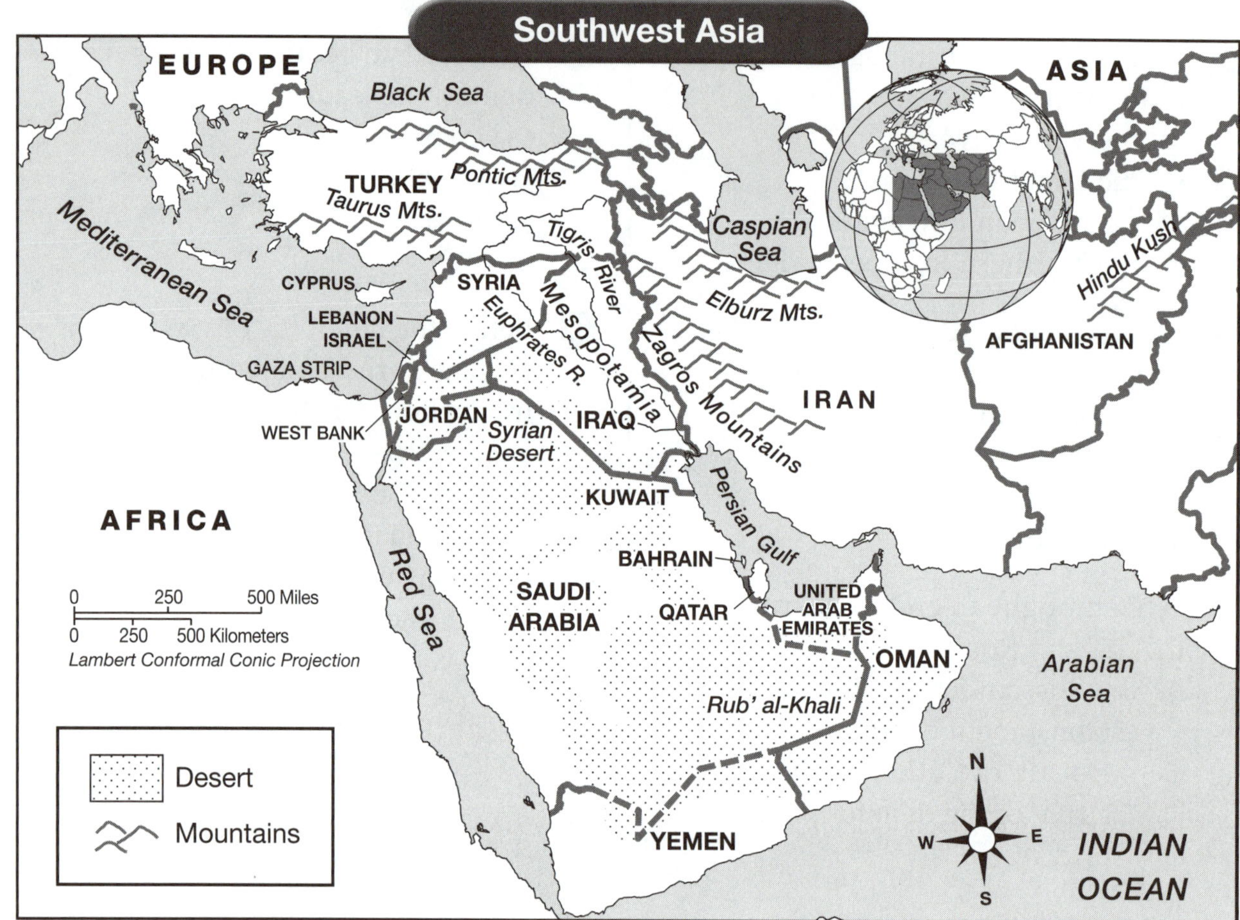

1. Southwest Asia has many different physical features and is more than a region of deserts. _Responses should include details about the region's mountain chains, rivers, and fertile plains. Details about the region's bodies of water may also be included._

2. Southwest Asia has many natural resources other than oil. _Responses should include the region's mineral deposits and may also discuss the scarce fresh water supply and the many kinds of crops grown using irrigation and dry farming techniques._

Southwest Asia Long Ago

Directions Read the statement about each historical event below. Use your textbook and other reference materials to help you find the year that each event occurred. Write the year of each event on the line provided.

__2500 B.C.__ Sargon creates the Akkadian Empire by capturing all the Mesopotamian city-states.

__37 B.C.__ The land that was once the kingdom of Israel falls under Roman control.

__3500 B.C.__ Sumerian communities grow into city-states.

__500 B.C.__ The Persian Empire reaches from Egypt to India.

__1750 B.C.__ By this date, Hammurabi has conquered much of Mesopotamia, forming the Babylonian Empire.

__331 B.C.__ Alexander the Great conquers the Persian Empire.

Directions Study the dates on the time line below. Place each event above in its correct place on the time line.

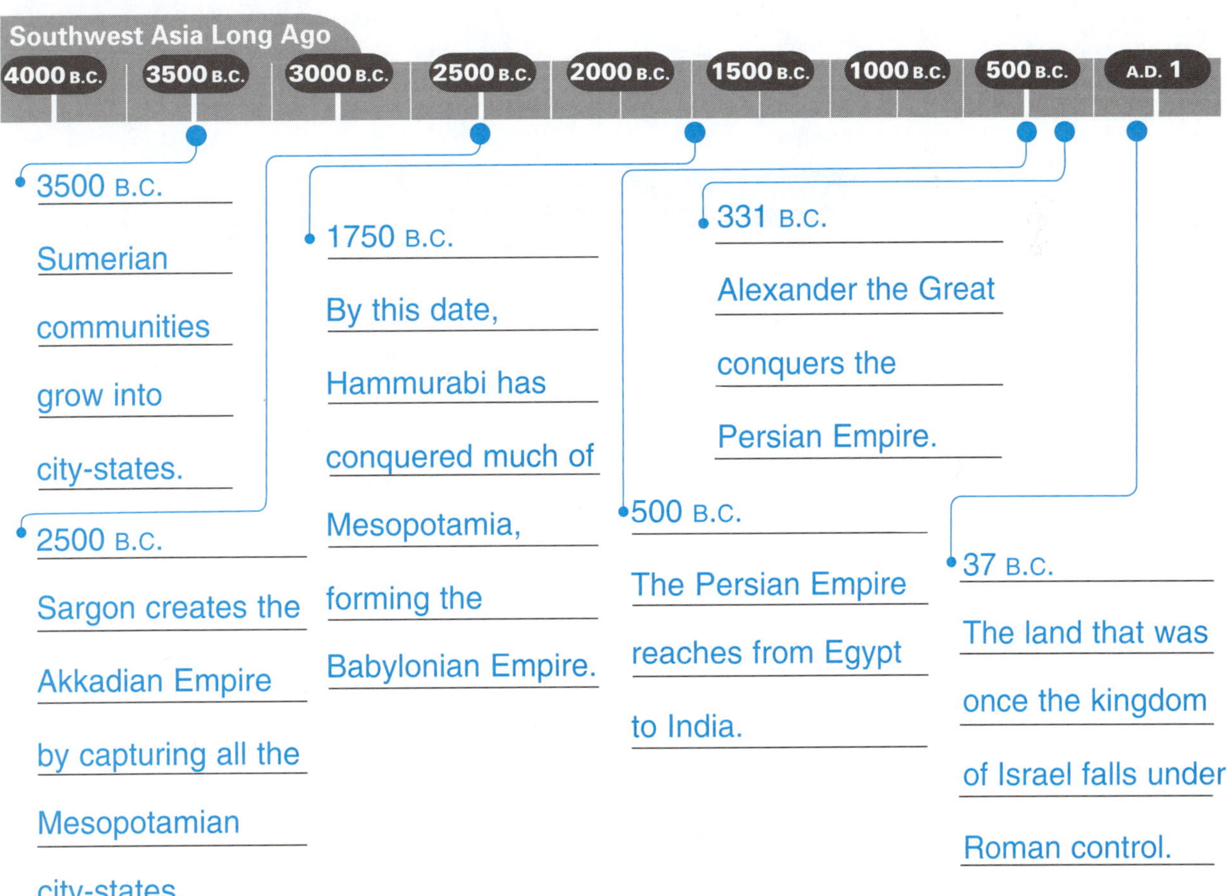

MAP AND GLOBE SKILLS

Compare Historical Maps

Directions   Study the maps below. Pay close attention to the information that they provide about Southwest Asia at different time periods. Use the maps to help you complete the activities that follow.

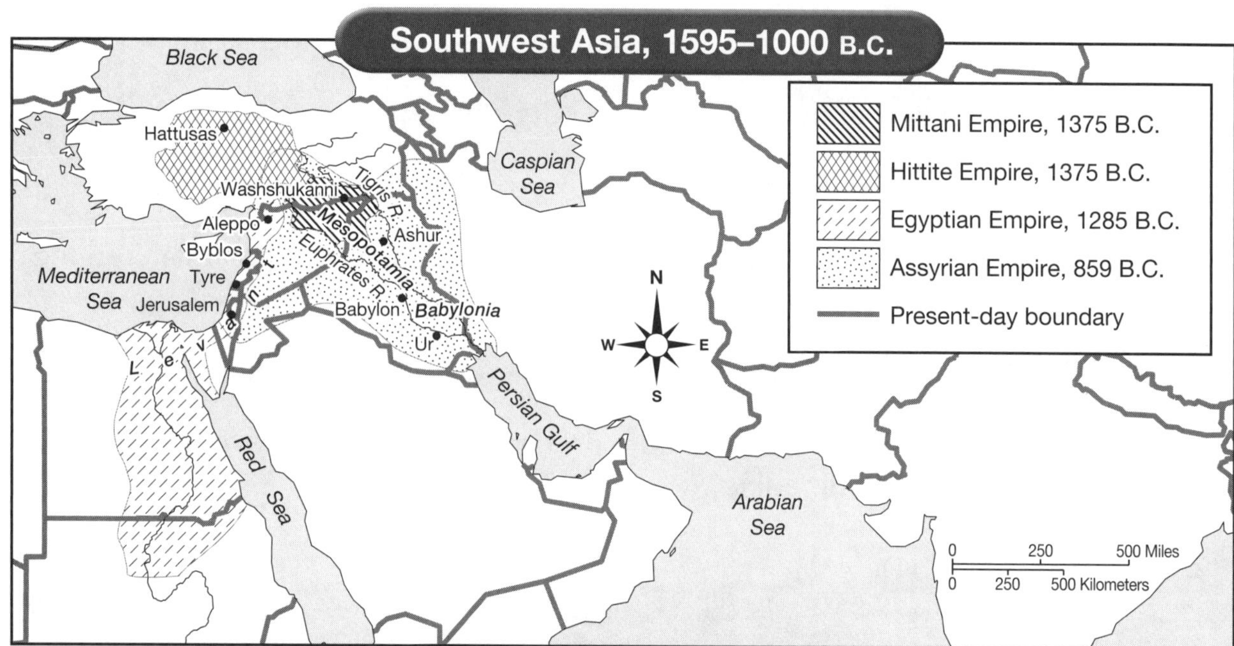

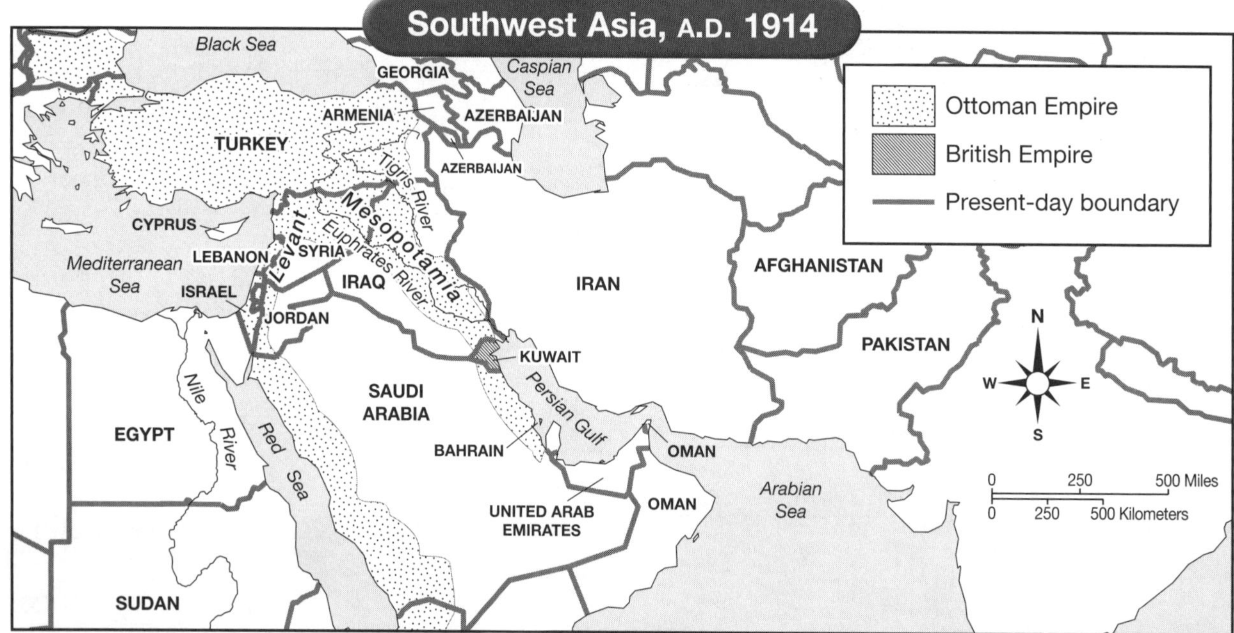

(continued)

Name _________________________________ Date _________________________

Directions **Study the empires shown on page 102. Then find the names of countries that today occupy the land that belonged to these empires. Write the names of these countries on the lines below the empires.**

1 Ottoman Empire

Turkey, Iraq, Syria, Lebanon, Israel, Jordan, Saudi Arabia

____

2 Assyrian Empire

Iraq, Kuwait, Turkey, Iran, Syria, Jordan, Israel

3 Mittani Empire

Syria, Iraq, Turkey

4 Hittite Empire

Turkey

5 Egyptian Empire

Egypt, Israel, Jordan, Lebanon, Syria, Sudan

Directions **Study the maps on page 102 to answer the following questions.**

6 Write the names of the empires that conquered Mesopotamia in historical order.

the Mittani Empire, the Assyrian Empire, and the Ottoman Empire

____

7 Which empire on the maps was the last to control the country of Jordan?

the Ottoman Empire

Influences on Cultures

Directions Read the following paragraph. Use the information in the paragraph and your textbook to complete the chart below.

Many different groups of people live in Southwest Asia. The majority of these people are Arabs. They live in several of the countries in the region. Other groups, including Afghans, Greeks, Jews, and Iranians, live in different parts of Southwest Asia. Many of the Arab and Iranian peoples are Muslims. They belong to either the Sunni or Shi'i branches of Islam. Other groups, such as the Greek people of Cyprus, are Christians. The majority of the people of Israel are Jewish. Israel is the only country in the region where Judaism is the official religion.

Countries of Southwest Asia			
Country	**Ethnic Group(s)**	**Religious Practice(s)**	**Major Language(s)**
Afghanistan	Afghans	Sunni Muslim, Shi'i Muslim	Dari, Pashto
Bahrain	Arabs	Sunni Muslim	Arabic
Cyprus	Greeks, Turks	Christian, Sunni Muslim	Greek
Iran	Iranians, Kurds	Shi'i Muslim	Farsi
Iraq	Arabs, Kurds	Sunni Muslim, Shi'i Muslim	Arabic
Israel	Jews, Palestinians	Jewish, Sunni Muslim, Christian	Hebrew
Jordan	Arabs, Palestinians	Sunni Muslim, Christian	Arabic
Kuwait	Arabs	Sunni Muslim	Arabic
Lebanon	Arabs	many Muslim and Christian sects	Arabic
Oman	Arabs	Sunni Muslim	Arabic
Qatar	Arabs	Sunni Muslim	Arabic
Saudi Arabia	Arabs	Sunni Muslim	Arabic
Syria	Arabs, Kurds	Sunni Muslim, Christian	Arabic
Turkey	Turks, Kurds	Sunni Muslim, Christian	Turkish
United Arab Emirates	Arabs	Sunni Muslim, Christian	Arabic
Yemen	Arabs	Sunni Muslim, Shi'i Muslim	Arabic

New Governments and Strong Economies

Directions In each statement, underline the name of the correct country. Use the chart showing oil production in Southwest Asia to choose the countries being described.

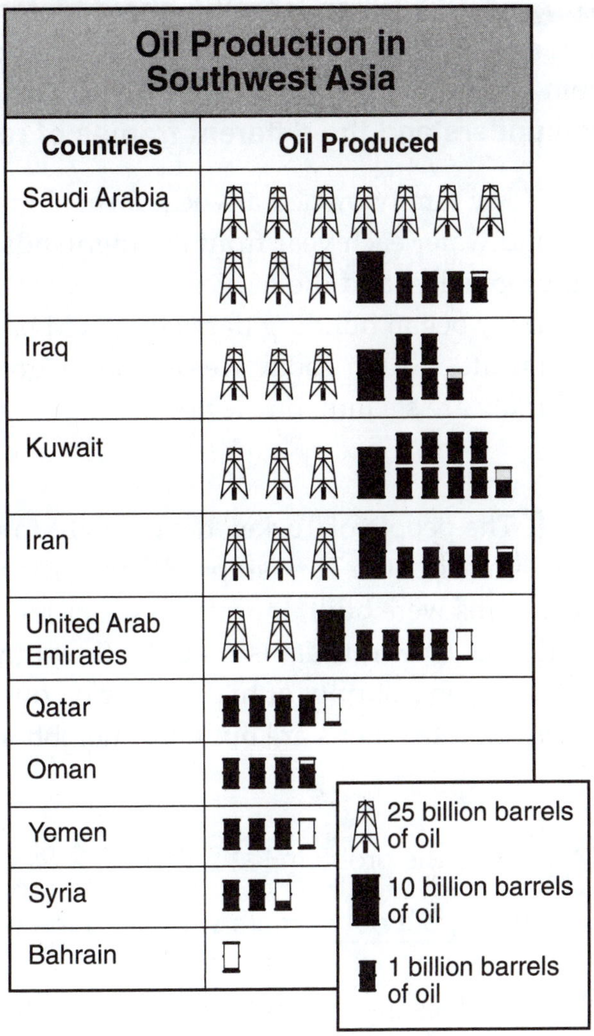

1 (<u>Kuwait</u>/Saudi Arabia) produces just over 93 billion barrels of oil. It produces slightly more than the country of Iraq.

2 Oman produces slightly more oil than this country, but not much more. (Iran/<u>Yemen</u>) totals just over 3 billion barrels of oil each year.

3 (<u>Iran</u>/Kuwait)'s almost 90 billion barrels of oil each year make it Southwest Asia's fourth-largest oil producer.

4 (<u>Bahrain</u>/Syria) produces the least amount of oil in the entire region of Southwest Asia.

Oil Production in Southwest Asia

Countries	Oil Produced
Saudi Arabia	
Iraq	
Kuwait	
Iran	
United Arab Emirates	
Qatar	
Oman	
Yemen	
Syria	
Bahrain	

Key:
- 25 billion barrels of oil
- 10 billion barrels of oil
- 1 billion barrels of oil

Directions Read the question. Write your answer on the lines provided.

5 Several countries in Southwest Asia belong to the Organization of Petroleum Exporting Countries (OPEC). How does being a member of OPEC help the countries?

Responses should include that OPEC provides scientific and economic aid for oil production and regulates the price of oil by limiting the amount of oil each country can produce.

READING SKILLS
Identify Frames of Reference

Directions When learning about historical events, it is important to study different frames of reference and points of view. Read each point of view about a dam project on the Euphrates River. Then answer the questions that follow to help you understand the different frames of references.

"My family owned a wheat farm along the Euphrates River. Floods brought rich soil and water each year from the highlands. We always had plenty of water to irrigate our crop fields, and the harvests were very large. Then in the 1960s and 1970s, the people of Turkey began building dams that held back the water. The river no longer floods and there is little water. Today we can barely grow enough food to survive. I think the people of Turkey are stealing our water."

A Syrian farmer

"The people of Turkey have a right to use the natural resources within our borders. The dams offer the Turkish people water for their crops and an energy supply. Before these dams were built, the river's water levels were high. Some years there were damaging floods. Now our dams keep the flow of water even at all times. They also give the whole region a supply of hydroelectric power. The other countries should be grateful. When all of the dams are built, our neighbors will see how the dams benefit us all."

A Turkish government official

1 What is the problem? The damming of the Euphrates River benefits the people of Turkey, but not farmers who need the water in Syria.

2 What does the Syrian farmer want? What does the Turkish government official want? The Syrian farmer wants to stop the damming of the Euphrates River. The Turkish official would like to see the dams completed.

3 What is the Syrian farmer's frame of reference? How does it affect his point of view? The Syrian farmer will not get any of the benefits from the dams. His job depends on water, so he believes that the dams should not be built.

4 What is the Turkish official's frame of reference. How does it affect his point of view? The Turkish official is from a country that gets benefits from the dams. He does not represent people in Syria. For that reason, he thinks the dams should be built.

Southwest Asia

Directions Complete this graphic organizer to show that you understand how to compare and contrast information about the influence of oil in Southwest Asia.

TOPIC A ______ ______	**TOPIC B** ______ ______

LIFE BEFORE THE DISCOVERY OF OIL

Students may mention that most people lived in rural areas.

People farmed and sold crops in markets.

Students may mention that few government services were available.

Food was sometimes in short supply.

LIFE AFTER THE DISCOVERY OF OIL

Urban areas and cities began to grow.

Students may mention that jobs in construction, manufacturing and service industries are increasing.

Governments were able to pay for improved health care and education.

Students may mention that money from the sale of oil made it possible to import food from countries with stronger agricultural industries.

Name _______________________________   Date _______________

Test Preparation

Directions   Read each question and choose the best answer. Then fill in the circle for the answer you have chosen. Be sure to fill in the circle completely.

1 The Tigris and Euphrates Rivers come together in southeastern Iraq to form the—
- (A) Shatt al Arab.
- (B) Rub'al-Khali.
- (C) Jordan River.
- (D) Kuwait River.

2 Southwest Asia is a crossroads where Asia and Africa meet another continent. What is the name of the third continent?
- (F) North America
- (G) South America
- (H) Europe
- (J) Australia

3 An ancient Sumerian city-state—
- (A) had a group of leaders.
- (B) had a temple called a ziggurat.
- (C) had a religion based on worshiping one God.
- (D) had no form of writing or language for record keeping.

4 Islamic laws discourage images of people or animals. Which image might be found in a piece of Islamic art?
- (F) coins and sword dancers
- (G) people relaxing on a beach
- (H) horses and bulls
- (J) geometric shapes

5 At the end of World War I, the Allied Powers took most of the defeated Ottoman Empire's land. The land left in Ottoman control became which country?
- (A) Israel
- (B) Syria
- (C) Turkey
- (D) Saudi Arabia

A Region of Deserts

Directions The geography of North Africa is harsh. Yet it is home to millions of people. Read each of the main ideas about the geography of North Africa. For each main idea, write three details that support it.

COASTAL PLAIN

The coastal plain is an ideal place for much of the region's population.

1. The plain has a mild climate (hot, dry summers and warm, wet winters).

2. The plain has fertile farmland.

3. The plain has access to the Mediterranean Sea.

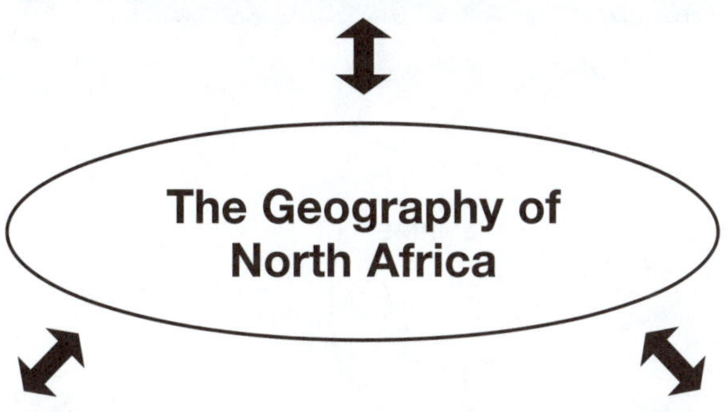

NILE RIVER

The Nile River is an important resource for the people of Egypt.

1. The Nile offers a constant water source.

2. A ribbon of rich, fertile soil lines the river.

3. River dams control the waters of the Nile and generate electricity.

THE SAHARA

The Sahara is mostly barren, but has some resources for the region's people.

1. The Sahara's oasis areas provide water for people to live.

2. People can turn desert oases into farmland.

3. People pipe the water from oases to the coastal plain.

Use after reading Chapter 12, Lesson 1, pages 400–405.

MAP AND GLOBE SKILLS
Follow Routes on a Map

Directions Study the map of the ancient trade routes of Egypt. Pay close attention to both the land and the water routes. Then use the map to help you complete the activities that follow.

Ancient Egypt traded with several other civilizations around the known world. Egyptian merchants exchanged goods with the Libyan peoples to the west, African civilizations in the south, and the empires of Southwest Asia and Europe. Merchants traveled land and water routes that crossed the world to bring goods such as gold, turquoise, and wood to Egyptian temples and the pharaoh's court.

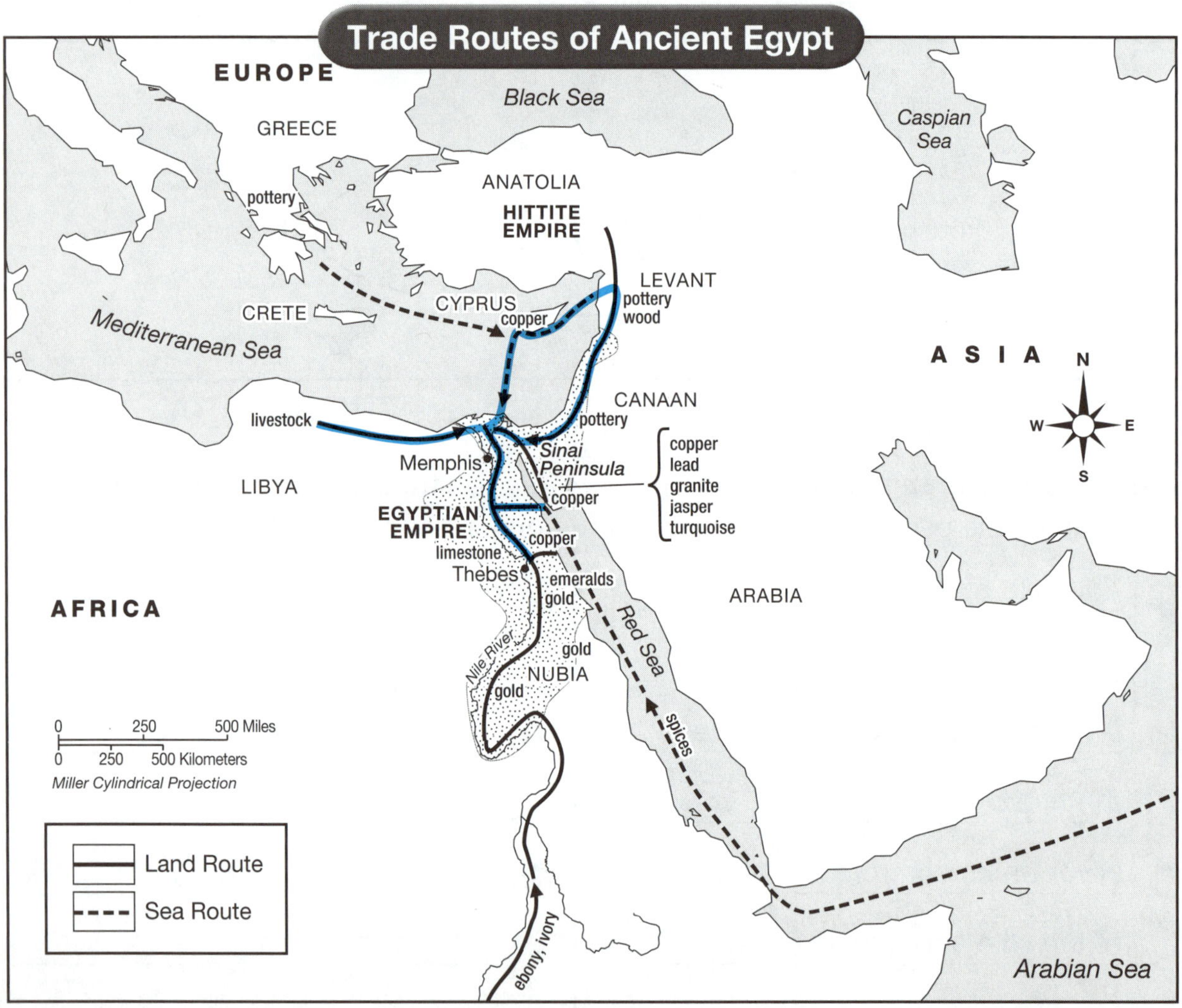

(continued)

                Use after reading Chapter 12, Skill Lesson, pages 406–407.

Name ____ Date _______________________

Directions Imagine you are an ancient Egyptian merchant. The pharaoh
needs several products for the royal temples and palaces at Thebes. Read the
list below. Then plan a trade mission to find the goods, using the shortest route
possible. Draw your route on the map, starting at Memphis. Then describe the
route in the space below.

Wood for the river barges	Horses to pull the royal chariots
Copper for royal mirrors and tools	Turquoise for jewelry

Students' descriptions will vary based on the routes they choose. Encourage

them to use both land and water routes.

____

____

____

Directions The pharaoh has demanded more goods. Study the map and
answer the questions to meet his needs.

1 Where might you find ebony for the pharaoh? to the south of Nubia

____

2 If you are in the city of Thebes, in which direction would you travel to find

the ebony? south

3 In which direction from Thebes would you find emeralds? east

4 If you were in the Nile Delta, how would you travel to find pottery for the

pharaoh's palaces? Both land and water routes will connect you to the pottery

markets in Canaan, the Levant, and Greece.

5 From the Nile Delta, where would you find the closest source of copper and

turquoise, and how might you get there? The closest source is the Sinai

Peninsula. One would take the land route that runs southeast from the delta

over the Sinai Peninsula.

Ancient Days to Independence

Directions The natural resources in and around the Nile River had many effects on life in ancient Egypt. Read each pair of statements about the Egyptian civilization. Decide which is the cause and which is the effect. Write the letter C (Cause) or E (Effect) on the lines to identify the statements.

1 __C__ The Nile River floods carried rich soils and inundated the land along the river bank.

__E__ Egyptian farmers planted and harvested crops in the rich soil along the river bank.

2 __E__ The Egyptians believed that they would live again after death.

__C__ The Egyptians saw the sun rise and fall and thought it was a god who was born each morning and died each night.

3 __E__ The Egyptian farmers worked on the pharaoh's building projects.

__C__ The Nile River floods covered the crop fields for weeks, preventing any planting.

4 __C__ Egypt became a wealthy nation because of its rich soil and many crops.

__E__ Egypt's enemies wanted to conquer the kingdom to control its resources.

Directions Some effects become the causes of other effects. Study each picture and read its statement. Determine if it could be the cause of another effect. Then number each of the statements in the order that they might occur as a series of causes and effects.

__5__ Tombs were built to house the objects a person would need in his or her afterlife.

__3__ The Egyptians believed they would have an afterlife.

__1__ The vegetation in the Nile Valley died after each harvest, and then the season changed.

__2__ The Nile Valley came back to life after each inundation.

__4__ The Egyptians developed ways of preserving dead bodies.

     Use after reading Chapter 12, Lesson 2, pages 408–413.

CHART AND GRAPH SKILLS
Read a Telescoping Time Line

Directions The time line below shows some of the key dates in the history of North Africa. One section of the time line has been expanded to help you take a closer look at events that happened in recent times. Use both parts of the time line to answer the questions on page 114.

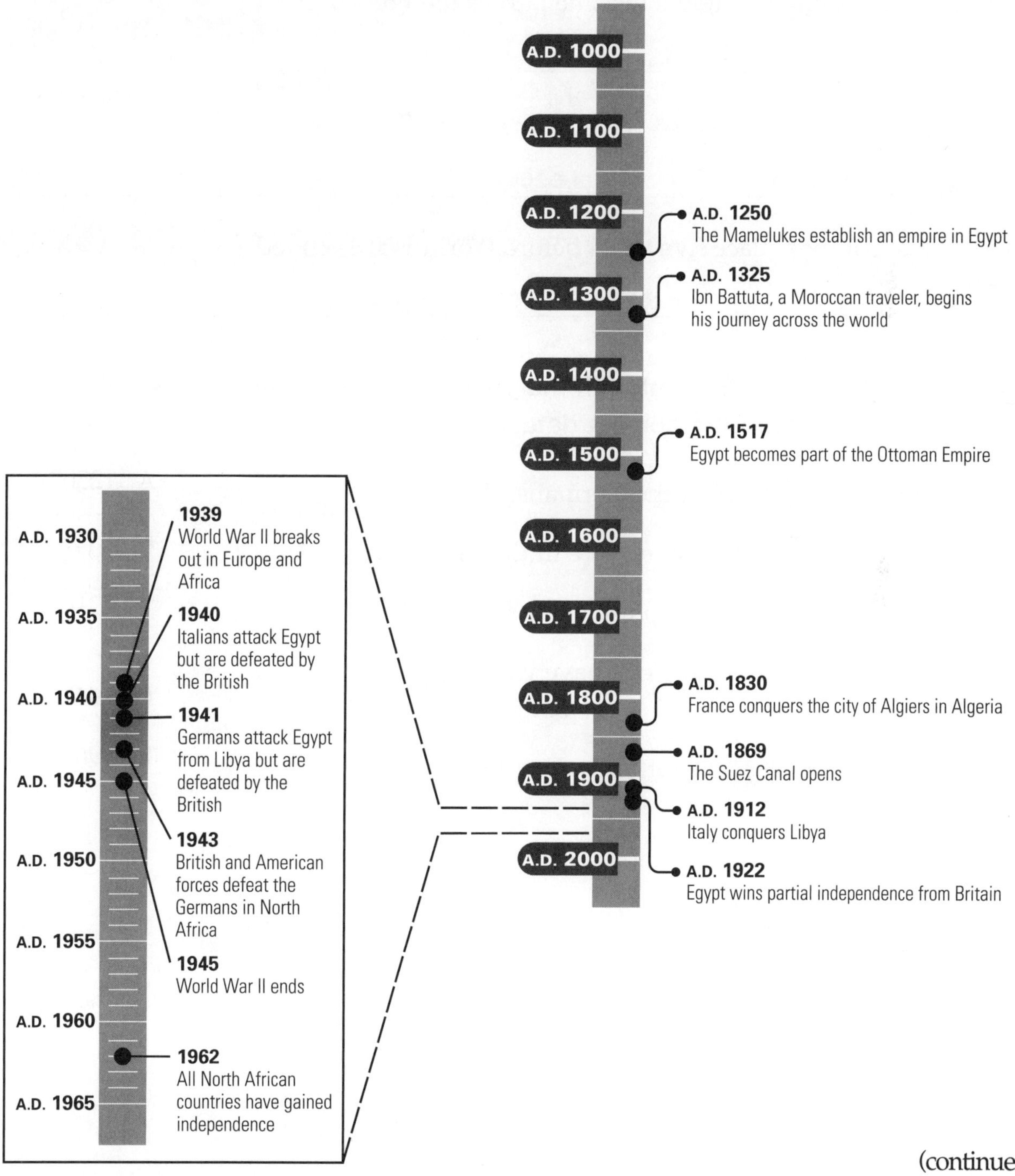

(continued)

Name ____ Date _______________

1 What time period does the time line show? What time period does the

telescoping part of the time line show? A.D. 1000 to A.D. 2000; A.D. 1930 to

A.D. 1965.

2 According to the time line, which group conquered Egypt first? How long did

they rule Egypt? the Mamelukes; 267 years

3 When did the city of Algiers become part of the French Empire?

1830

4 Which event took place first, the opening of the Suez Canal or the Italian

conquest of Libya? The Suez canal opened first, in 1869.

5 Which event took place five years before World War II ended?

The Italians attacked Egypt and were defeated by the British.

Directions **Match each event with the year that it took place. Draw a line connecting the event to the correct date.**

6 The British in Egypt defeat the Germans.   **A.** 1250

7 The Mamelukes establish an empire in Egypt.   **B.** 1325

8 Ibn Battuta leaves Morocco to travel the world.   **C.** 1517

9 All the countries of North Africa have won
independence.   **D.** 1941

10 Egypt becomes part of the Ottoman Empire.   **E.** 1962

A Blend of Cultures

Directions Anthropologists are people who study the societies and cultures of other peoples. Imagine that you are an anthropologist traveling in North Africa to study either a Berber or Bedouin group. Write a journal entry that describes what it is like to live with one of these groups. Make sure your journal answers the questions below.

1. Where does your group live? Draw a map in the box to the right that shows its location.

2. What languages do the people in your group speak?

3. How is the group's way of life different from other ways of life in the region?

4. How has your group resisted changes to the region that were brought by conquerors?

5. How has your group adapted to new ideas and innovations brought by other cultures?

1. Students' maps may illustrate countries or desert regions in North Africa where the Berber people live or the Sinai Peninsula where many Bedouin people are found. 2. Students should describe Arabic and Berber as languages that are spoken equally by both tribes. 3. Students' responses may mention that their people are Muslims; students may provide details concerning Islamic religious practices. However, some of the people may also continue practicing the traditional religions of the region. 4. Answers may include the continuity of the group's nomadic lifestyle, traditional religious practices, and occupation as herders. 5. Possible answers include the adoption of Islam as their religion and Arabic as their language, as well as the building of permanent homes.

Present-Day Concerns

Directions Almanacs are sources of information about all the countries of the world. People use almanacs because they contain the most current information about governments, culture, and history. People also use almanacs for up-to-date information about countries' economies. Use the almanac information below to help you answer the questions about Morocco's economy.

Population: over 30 million people

Labor Force: 11 Million

Percentage of agricultural workers: 50%

Percentage of industrial and service workers: 45%

Industrial and Service Products: Phosphates, foods, leather, and textiles; tourism and construction

Agricultural Products: Barley, wheat, citrus, wine, vegetables, olives, and livestock

Area: 172,413 sq. miles or 446,515 sq. km

Trading Partners: France, Germany, India, Italy, Japan, Spain, and the United States

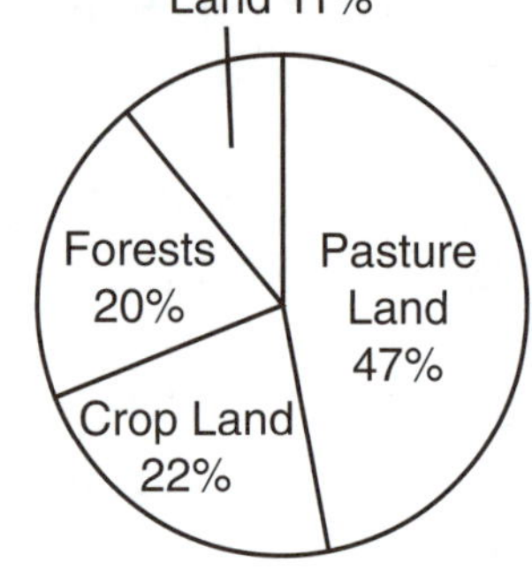

1 What kinds of jobs do most of Morocco's workers have?

agricultural jobs

2 What kinds of products do these Moroccan workers produce?

They produce barley, wheat, citrus, wine, vegetables, olives, and livestock.

3 Study the land use graph. How much land is used to produce these products? 69% of the land

4 How would you describe the economy of Morocco? Student's answers may include an idea of the Moroccan economy being a mixed economy. The Moroccan economy has agriculture and industry. In addition, the workforce, land, and products are divided almost evenly between agricultural and industrial products.

North Africa

Directions Complete this graphic organizer to show that you understand how to sequence events in the history of Egypt.

FIRST → **NEXT** → **LAST**

In 525 B.C. Persians conquer Egypt and rule it for 200 years.

↓

In 332 B.C. Alexander the Great conquers Egypt.

↓

About 31 B.C. The Romans defeat Cleopatra and take control of Egypt.

↓

In A.D. 395 Egypt becomes part of the Byzantine Empire.

About A.D. 643 Arab Muslims invade North Africa.

↓

In A.D. 1798 the French take control of Egypt.

↓

In the early A.D. 1800s Britain gains control of Egypt.

↓

In A.D. 1922 Britain gives Egypt limited self-rule.

12 Test Preparation

Directions Read each question and choose the best answer. Then fill in the circle for the answer you have chosen. Be sure to fill in the circle completely.

1 Most of the people in North Africa live in the—
- Ⓐ Coastal Plains.
- Ⓑ Tell Atlas.
- Ⓒ Sahara.
- Ⓓ Libyan Desert.

2 How does the Suez Canal benefit the people of North Africa and the world?
- Ⓕ It provides fresh drinking water to the Libyan coast.
- Ⓖ It links the Nile River to the Red Sea.
- Ⓗ It helps ships travel from the Mediterranean Sea to the Indian Ocean without going around Africa.
- Ⓙ It helps ships avoid the Nile cataracts and reach Lake Victoria in East Africa.

3 People flocked to North Africa's cities in modern times—
- Ⓐ to find small apartments.
- Ⓑ to find jobs or an education.
- Ⓒ to live on rooftops or boats.
- Ⓓ to preach Christianity.

4 What effect did the European conquest have on North Africa's countries?
- Ⓕ Europeans introduced Arabic laws and traditions into North Africa.
- Ⓖ Europeans influenced the laws and legal traditions of North Africa.
- Ⓗ Conquest helped the North Africans discover oil.
- Ⓙ The Europeans brought Islam into North Africa.

5 Which is one reason why European countries are North Africa's main trading partners?
- Ⓐ North African countries are colonies of European countries.
- Ⓑ North African goods are inexpensive.
- Ⓒ The European countries are very close to North Africa.
- Ⓓ Both Europeans and North Africans are Muslims.

                                       Use after reading Chapter 12, pages 398–429.

Desert, Savanna, and Rain Forest

The three climate and vegetation regions in West and Central Africa have shaped the economies of the region's countries. The Sahel is an almost lifeless plain of sand dunes and gravel that borders the Sahara Desert in the north. The Sahel has little rainfall and long periods of drought. Few people live in this region. Its farmers grow dry-climate crops such as peanuts, cotton, millet, and sorghum. To the south of the Sahel is the savanna region. This is a region of flat plains and tall grasses. During the rainy season, farmers of the savanna grow such crops as potatoes, onions, corn, and yams. Large plantations in the savanna also grow such crops as coffee and cacao beans to be sold on the world market. Further south are the hot and wet rain forests. This region is the site of dense forests with few farms. Lumber, minerals, rubber, fruits, and fossil fuels are produced in this region.

Countries and Products of West and Central Africa			
Countries	**Products**	**Countries**	**Products**
Benin	beans, cassava, corn, cotton, rice, sorghum, palm products, peanuts, and petroleum	Burkina Faso	cattle, corn, cotton, goats, millet, peanuts, petroleum, rice, shea nuts, sheep, and sorghum
Cameroon	bananas, cassava, cocoa, coffee, cotton, millet, palm products, peanuts, petroleum, plantains, rubber, sorghum, tobacco, and yams	Chad	cassava, cotton, millet, peanuts, rice, sorghum, and yams
Democratic Republic of the Congo	cassava, coffee, corn, cotton, palm products, plantains, rice, rubber, tea, sugarcane, and yams	Gabon	cocoa, petroleum, and woods (okume, mahogany, ebony)
Mali	cassava, corn, cotton, millet, peanuts, rice, and sorghum	Niger	camels, cassava, cattle, cotton, cow peas, goats, millet, onions, peanuts, poultry, rice, sheep, and sorghum

(continued)

Directions Use the table on page 119 to help you identify the correct African country for each numbered item. Fill in the name of the country on the line provided.

1 Cocoa, coffee, cotton, and petroleum are four of the many products this Central African country produces. This country is called
________________Cameroon________________ .

2 The country of ________________Niger________________ produces many subsistence crops, such as millet, cassava, and rice. The people of this country also raise goats, sheep, and camels.

3 Millet, cotton, peanuts, sorghum and other dry-climate crops are grown in
________________Mali________________ and ________________Chad________________ , two West African countries located in the Sahel.

4 Sugarcane is a product of ________the Democratic Republic of the Congo________ , a large Central African country.

5 Woods and petroleum are major products of ________________Gabon________________ .

6 The country of ________________Burkina Faso________________ produces many products, including shea nuts, livestock, and petroleum.

Directions Study the crops and minerals produced in each country. Use the information to help you choose the correct climate and vegetation region found in each country.

7 Exotic woods, cacao, and petroleum are found in Gabon. What type of climate and vegetation region is located in Gabon? ________rain forest________

8 Niger has two climate and vegetation regions where crops such as millet, peanuts, potatoes, and onions are grown. What kinds of regions are located in Niger?
________the Sahel and savanna________

     Use after reading Chapter 13, Lesson 1, pages 444–449.

MAP AND GLOBE SKILLS
Compare Map Projections

Directions Read the paragraph and study the map projections below. Use the maps and your textbook to help you answer the questions that follow.

Mapmakers, or cartographers, have developed several ways to show the round Earth on flat maps. These different ways are called projections. Each projection has its own distortions of the landforms and bodies of water on Earth. Equal-area projection maps show correct sizes of landforms, but the shapes are distorted. Conformal projection maps show directions correctly but alter the sizes of landforms and bodies of water. Cartographers think about these distortions when choosing maps for certain purposes.

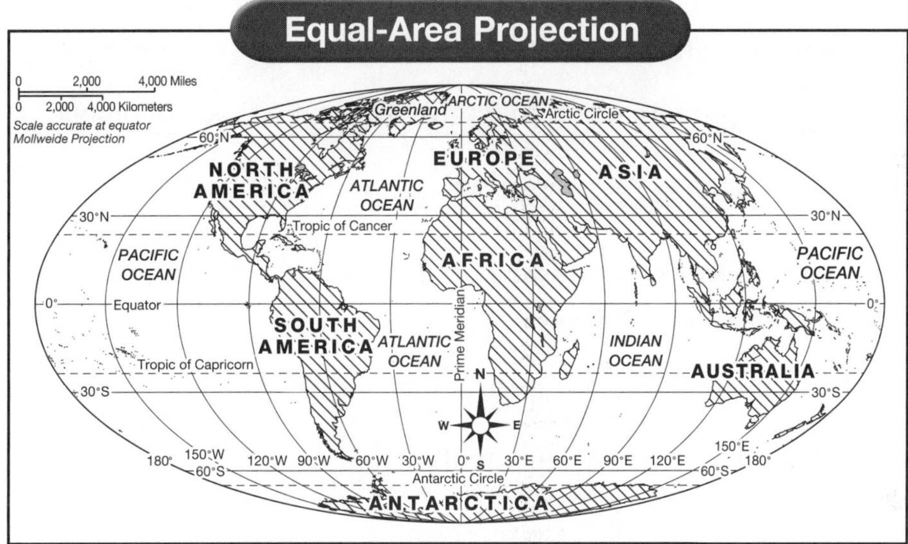

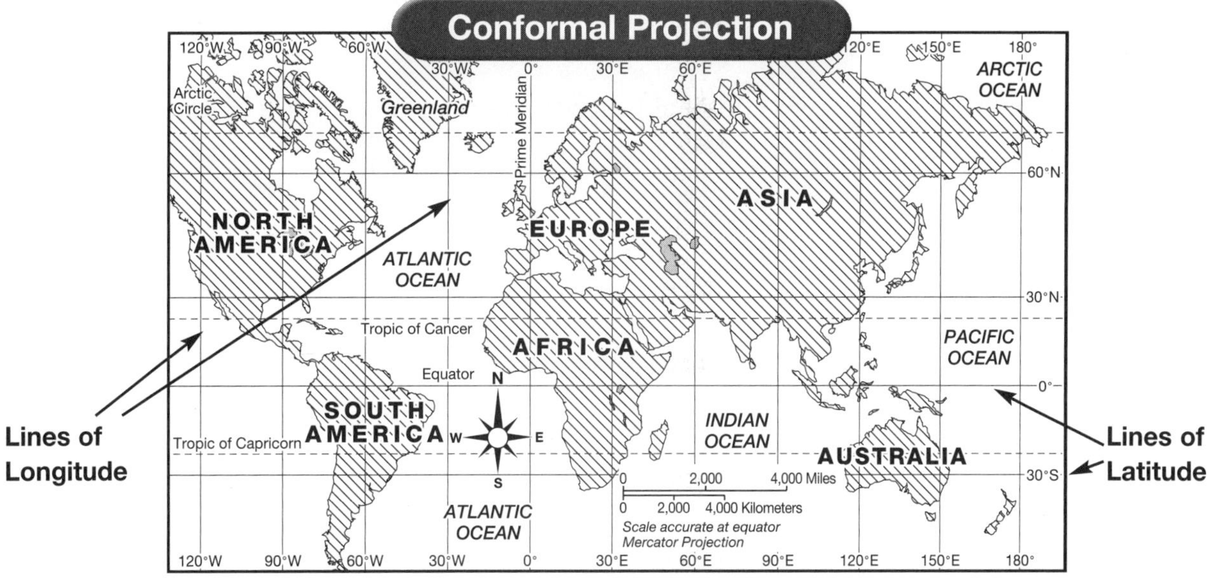

(continued)

Name ____ Date ____________________

1 Which map projection would a cartographer use to study the shape of Africa?
the conformal projection

2 Which projection might be used to study the correct size of Antarctica?
the equal-area projection

3 Which map projection might be used to determine the direction of Africa from
South America? the conformal projection

4 To compare the sizes of Madagascar and Iceland, a cartographer might use which
map projection? the equal-area projection

5 If a cartographer were studying the size of Greenland, why would a conformal
projection not be used? The conformal projection distorts sizes of landforms,
especially near the poles.

Directions **Study the maps on page 121. Then circle the correct word to
complete the sentences that follow.**

6 North America appears (larger /(smaller)) on the equal-area projection.

7 The lines of longitude are ((equal)/ unequal) distances apart on a
conformal projection.

8 Africa and South America are ((closer)/ more distant) on an equal-area
projection map.

9 On a conformal projection, the lines of latitude are (closer to /(more distant from))
each other near the poles.

A Time of Empires

Directions **West Africa has been the location of many powerful empires. Read the paragraph and study the map to help you answer the questions that follow.**

The West African empires of Ghana, Mali, and Songhai controlled an area of busy trade routes. As the empires grew, they captured the trading cities located between West Africa and the Mediterranean region. Cities such as Timbuktu, Jenné, and Walata grew rich from the exchange of gold, salt, and slaves. In the busy markets of these cities, caravans carrying salt from North Africa traded their goods for the gold and other products of West Africa's coastal regions.

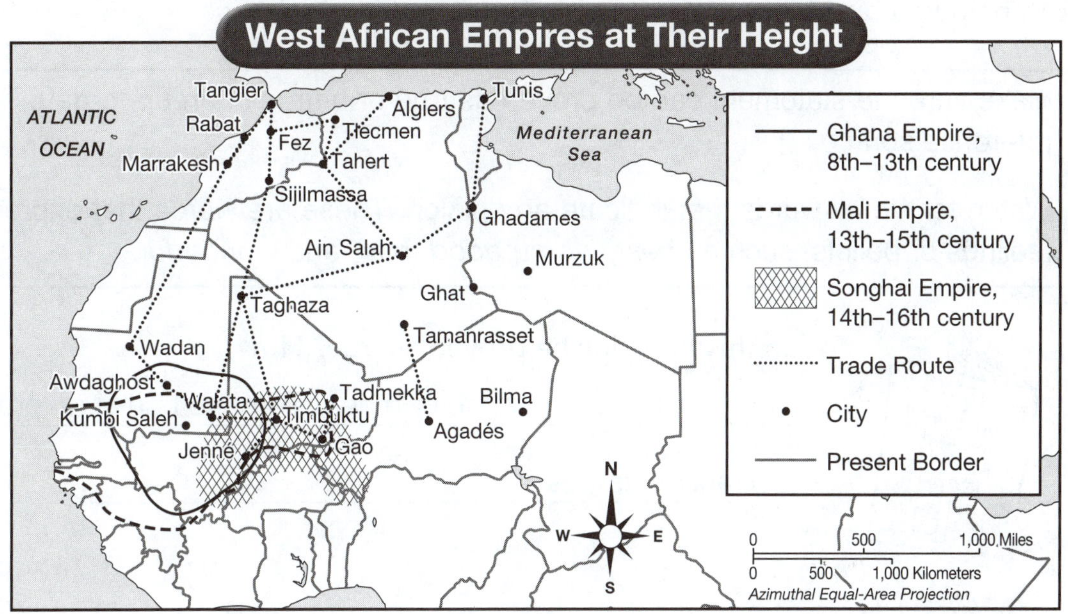

1 Which empire was established first and at its height controlled the cities of Walata and Kumbi Saleh? Ghana

2 Which empire rose to power as the empire of Ghana crumbled? Mali

3 If a caravan left Tangier and traveled due south to Jenné, which cities would it have passed through on the journey? Fez, Sijilmassa, Taghaza, and Timbuktu

4 Which empire was the larger in land area, Ghana or Mali?

The empire of Ghana was larger in land area.

5 A caravan passing through the city of Timbuktu in the year 1320 would have been visiting which empire? Mali

READING SKILLS
Identify Fact and Opinion

Directions **Read the tips for identifying facts and opinions. Then use the tips to help answer the questions that follow.**

Every day we read facts and opinions in newspapers, books, and on the Internet. Identifying facts and opinions can sometimes be difficult. Facts are statements that can be proven as true. An opinion is a statement that expresses someone's belief or feelings about a topic. Remember to follow these steps when you read statements. They can help you decide if a statement is a fact or an opinion.

> - Make sure the statement can be proven as true or untrue in an up-to-date reference source.
>
> - Watch for signal words that indicate an opinion. These are words that express feelings or beliefs, such as *best, worst, good, bad,* and *wonderful*.

1  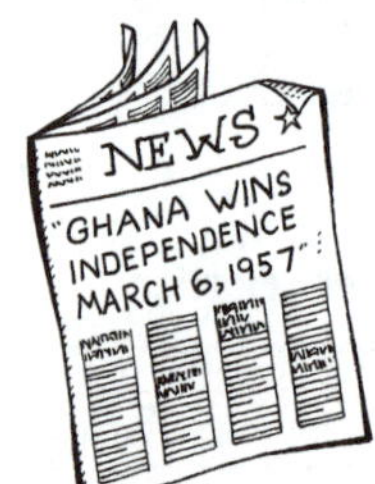

Can this headline be proven as true? How?

Yes. Checking an almanac or other reference book can prove the headline as true.

2  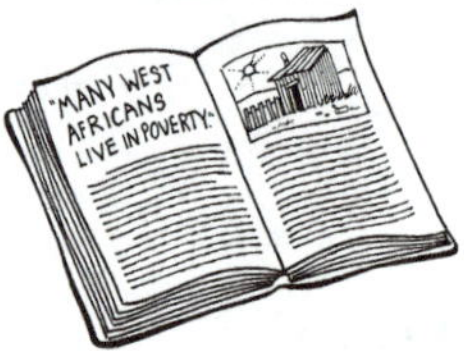

Is the statement "Many West Africans Live in Poverty" a fact or an opinion? How do you know?

It is a fact. Facts can be proven with up-to-date reference materials. One can prove the statement by researching data about West Africa.

3  

How do you know this statement is an opinion and not a fact?

It is an opinion that expresses someone's feelings or belief that cannot be proven as true or untrue. The word *best* is a clue that an opinion is being expressed

Many Cultures

Directions Read the passages about African culture below. Then paraphrase, or write in your own words, the main idea of each passage.

1 Historians believe that groups of West African farmers speaking a language called Bantu migrated throughout West and Central Africa. As the farmers moved into new areas, they spread their language, agriculture, and tools. The languages of people in West and Central Africa have many similarities. Today, many of these languages continue to have several of the same words.

Many languages in West and Central Africa are related to a language

called Bantu that was spread by migrating West African farmers.

2 Many African countries are home to many different ethnic groups. These countries' ethnic groups each have distinct languages. It is possible for African countries to have dozens of different languages spoken within their borders. The people in these countries also speak European languages introduced during the colonial period. All the ethnic groups in these countries speak a European language. The European languages are often the countries' official languages.

Many countries use a European language as their official language because

they have many different ethnic groups that speak different languages.

3 In Chad and Mauritania, European languages are not official languages. Arab traders first reached these countries in the 700s. They spread Islam and the Arabic language to West Africa. Today, many African Muslims in Chad and Mauritania learn Arabic as part of their religious education. Arabic is an official language in

both countries. Arabic is an official language in both Chad and Mauritania.

4 Many African languages are spoken by small ethnic groups. Some groups have fewer than 1,000 people. As the people of these ethnic groups are entered into larger cultural groups, their languages change and disappear. Someday these languages

may disappear altogether. Many small African ethnic groups and their

languages are disappearing as they become part of larger groups.

Name ____   Date _________________

Developing Nations

 Many African countries gained their independence from European colonial empires after World War II. The newly-independent countries were faced with many problems. Study the list of problems. Then match the problems to the colonial characteristics that caused them. Write the problems on the lines under the matching colonial characteristics.

African workers became economically dependent on European trade. African countries lacked skilled workers and managers. African countries were made up of many different ethnic groups that did not unite into a single nation.	African governments became corrupt. African countries were autocracies or were ruled by the military. African roads and railroads were in poor condition. African economies were based on exporting a single crop or product.

Colonial Characteristics

European colonists in Africa raised cash crops and mined minerals for sale in Europe.

African workers became

economically dependent on

European trade.

African roads and railroads

were in poor condition.

African economies were based on

exporting a single crop or product.

____

____

Colonial governments did little to train the Africans for independence.

African countries lacked skilled

workers and managers.

African governments became

corrupt.

African countries were made up

of many different ethnic groups

that did not unite into a single

nation.

African countries were autocracies

or were ruled by the military.

                Use after reading Chapter 13, Lesson 4, pages 468–473.

Name ____ Date ________________

West and Central Africa

Directions Complete this graphic organizer to show that you understand how to summarize key points about West and Central Africa.

KEY POINTS

SUMMARY

LESSON 1: KEY POINTS

Possible response: Deserts, savannas, and rain forests are the three main climate and vegetation regions.

LESSON 1: SUMMARY

Students should mention differences between the Sahel, the savanna, and the rain forests.

LESSON 2: KEY POINTS

Possible response: Trade helped rulers in West and Central Africa build powerful empires.

LESSON 2: SUMMARY

Students may mention trading empires; the slave trade; the region's natural resources; the influence of European nations.

LESSON 3: KEY POINTS

Possible response: There is rich diversity in West and Central African cultures.

LESSON 3: SUMMARY

Students may mention different ethnic groups; lack of common languages; different religions; common belief in the importance of family.

LESSON 4: KEY POINTS

Possible response: West and Central Africans face problems as they work for economic independence and political stability.

LESSON 4: SUMMARY

Students may mention that profits during the colonial period were not invested in Africa; many African countries still remain in poverty; many unsuccessful forms of government.

Use after reading Chapter 13, pages 442–475.

13 Test Preparation

Directions Read each question and choose the best answer. Then fill in the circle for the answer you have chosen. Be sure to fill in the circle completely.

1 What is the Sahel?
- Ⓐ a region of West Africa that lies next to the rain forests
- Ⓑ a region of West Africa that is a transition zone between the desert and the grasslands
- Ⓒ a region of West Africa that is hot and wet
- Ⓓ a region of West Africa that has fertile farmlands

2 Many languages in West and Central Africa are related. The word that means "people" in these languages is—
- Ⓕ twi.
- Ⓖ bantu.
- Ⓗ hausa.
- Ⓙ lingala.

3 Which minerals are found in large amounts in the Democratic Republic of the Congo?
- Ⓐ bauxite and petroleum
- Ⓑ natural gases and zinc
- Ⓒ diamonds and gold
- Ⓓ bauxite and iron ore

4 Most African folktales are handed down orally and are about—
- Ⓕ singers and storytellers.
- Ⓖ music and dancing.
- Ⓗ heroes, common people, or animals.
- Ⓙ colonialism.

5 The African people faced many problems after independence, including—
- Ⓐ the Organization of African Unity.
- Ⓑ organizations that promoted economic development.
- Ⓒ colonial governments.
- Ⓓ little money to build industries.

Plains and Plateaus

Directions Study the map of East and Southern Africa. Note the locations of the region's deserts, mountains, lakes, and rivers. Use the map to help you answer the questions on page 130.

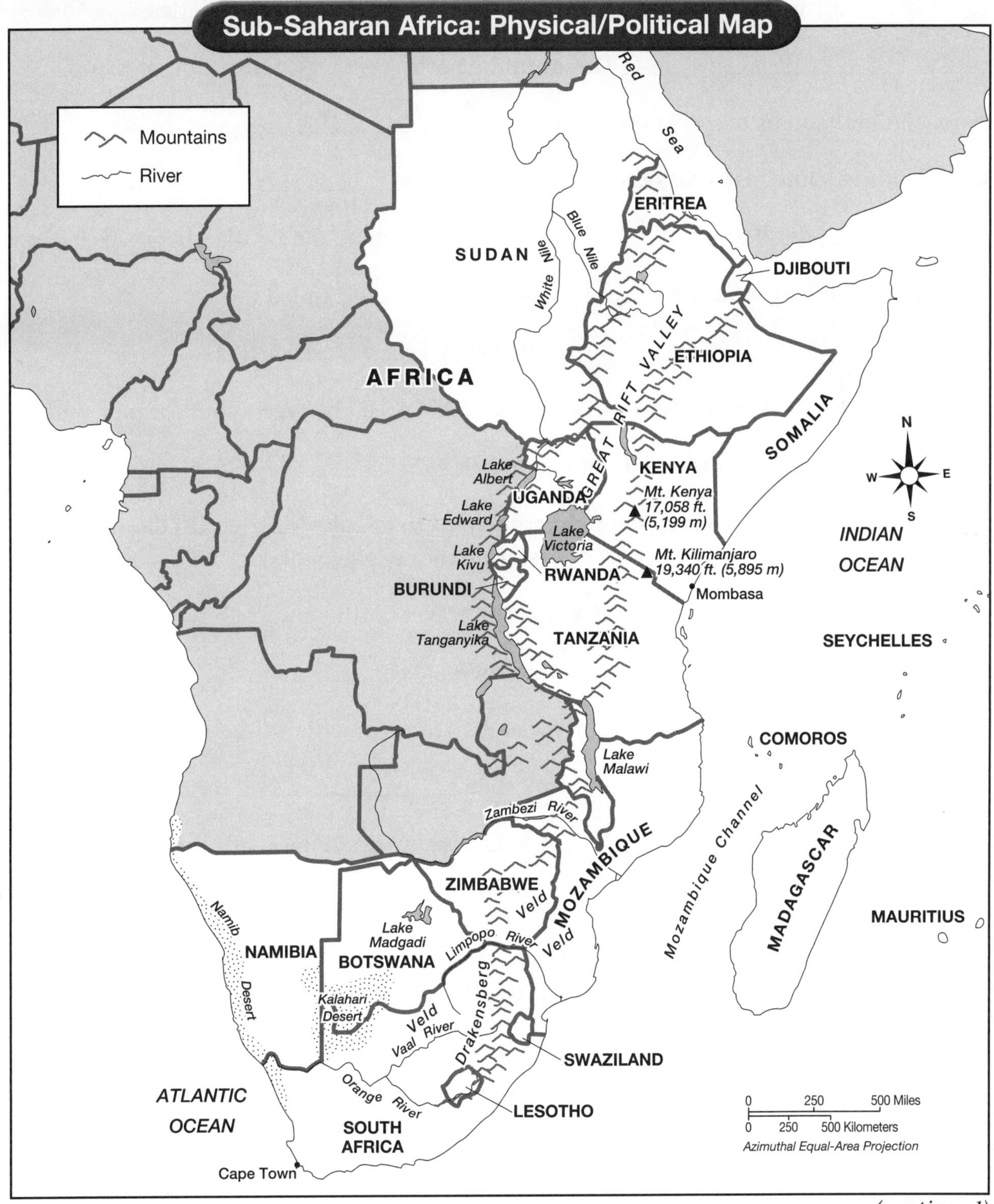

(continued)

Name ____ Date ________________________

 To many explorers Africa seemed like a mysterious continent. High cliffs, deep lakes, and vast grasslands challenged early explorers. Now it is your turn to travel this vast continent and study its unique geography. Read the paragraph below and fill in the missing places. Use the map on page 129 and your textbook to help you complete the trip.

1 Start your trip in Cape Town, South Africa. Head to the almost waterless

_______________ Namib _______________ Desert in the northwest. **2** Turn due east and

cross another famous desert known as the _______________ Kalahari _______________.

3 Heading southeast, cross the _______________ Vaal _______________ River and

the _______________ Orange _______________ River before reaching the Drakensberg

Mountains. **4** Turn northeast and cross a vast grassland called the

_______________ Veld _______________ by South Africa's early Dutch settlers.

5 Continuing northeast, begin traveling along the coast. Between your location and

the island of Madagascar is a body of water called the _______________ Mozambique Channel _______________.

6 Now circle northwest through Kenya, then south to Lake Malawi. On the way, cross
the mountainous terrain that is part of eastern Africa's large valley called

_______________ the Great Rift Valley _______________. **7** As you travel north, you reach two more lakes,

Lake _______________ Tanganyika _______________ and then Lake _______________ Victoria _______________.

8 Now move to the east and pass between two large mountains. Looking through

your guidebook, you realize that they are called _______________ Mount Kenya _______________

and _______________ Mount Kilimanjaro _______________. **9** End your trip in the coastal city to the

southeast. This famous city is called _______________ Mombasa _______________.

 Review the completed paragraph above. On a separate sheet of paper, describe another trip through southern and eastern Africa. Have a classmate travel through Africa by following your directions.

                    Use after reading Chapter 14, Lesson 1, pages 478–484.

Ancient Cultures

Directions Powerful kingdoms and centers of trade grew up in East and Southern Africa. Study the pictures and read each of the facts concerning these civilizations. Decide which civilization each fact describes. Then write the name of the correct civilization on the line next to each fact.

Kingdom of Kush

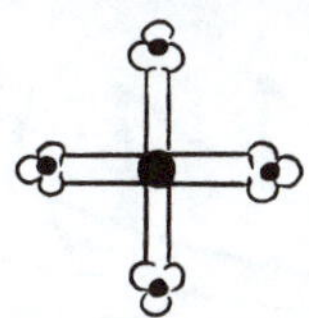

Axumite Empire

The Great Zimbabwe

Swahili City-States

1 _______The Great Zimbabwe_______ An empire that was established on a plateau south of the Zambezi River. The capital of the empire was a large walled city.

2 _______Axumite Empire_______ The empire expanded to include much of the Horn of Africa and even conquered Yemen on the Arabian Peninsula.

3 _______The Great Zimbabwe_______ The empire grew powerful by mining and trading the gold found in the region.

4 _______The Kingdom of Kush_______ The people of this empire were skilled ironworkers and had an agricultural industry that included cotton and flax.

5 _______Axumite Empire_______ The empire converted to Christianity and became an important center of Christian learning.

6 _______Swahili City-States_______ Arab merchants intermarried with Bantu peoples and established cities along the East African coast.

7 _______Axumite Empire_______ Within the empire was a busy port named Adulis, where Africans traded ivory, gold, and slaves for Mediterranean wine, olive oil, iron, and brass tools.

8 _______Swahili City-States_______ The merchants of this civilization traded with Arab merchants and the people of the African interior.

9 _______The Kingdom of Kush_______ The kingdom was influenced by the Egyptian civilization during its many years of close contact with the Egyptian Empire.

10 _______Swahili City-States_______ The richest cities of this civilization, such as Dar es Salaam, had large mosques, palaces, and homes.

From Colonies to Countries

Directions Imagine that you are a newspaper reporter covering the struggle for freedom in Tanzania and South Africa. On a separate sheet of paper, write a short article that compares the independence movements in both countries. Include in your article the list of events and details below. Remember to start the article with an interesting headline and answer the questions Who? What? When? Where? and How?

South Africa

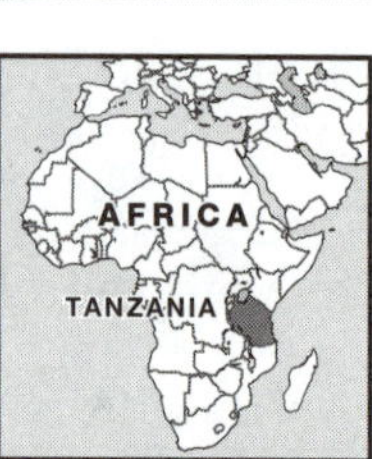

- Europeans, later known as Afrikaaners, settled South Africa in the seventeenth century.
- South Africa became part of Britain.
- In 1910, South Africa became independent of the British Empire.
- The African National Congress (ANC) fought to gain rights for Africans.
- In 1948, the National Party came to power and established apartheid.
- Violent protests by native Africans led the government to declare the ANC illegal.
- Nelson Mandela and other ANC leaders were arrested and imprisoned.
- From the mid 1970s until the late 1980s, other countries isolated South Africa.
- In 1989, South Africans voted to reform the government.
- In 1994, Nelson Mandela became the President of South Africa.

Tanzania

- Tanganyika had many European settlers.
- The colony had a well-organized nationalist movement headed by Julius Nyerere.
- Julius Nyerere united over 120 ethnic groups.
- The European settlers supported the country's new constitution.
- Tanganyika gained independence in 1958 and united with the island of Zanzibar in 1963.
- The two countries formed the new country of Tanzania.

     Use after reading Chapter 14, Lesson 3, pages 492–498.

Facing the Future

Directions Political stability and economic independence are issues facing East and Southern Africa today. The information in this lesson is presented in four sections. Use your textbook to answer the question for each section.

Economic Development

1 How might the economies of the East and Southern African countries be described? The economies of the region's countries have experienced little growth. With the exception of South Africa, Mauritius, and Botswana, most countries and their people are very poor.

Health and Welfare

2 Why do many East and Southern African countries have difficulty providing health care and education to their citizens? Political instability and poverty make it difficult for the governments of the region to provide health care services and educational opportunities to their people.

Protecting the Environment

3 How is deforestation changing the countries of East and Southern Africa? Deforestation causes fertile soils to wash away, deserts to grow, and valuable trees and tree products to disappear.

Culture and Conflict

4 What problems arose in a country with more than one cultural group? Answers may vary but should include details about the ethnic violence between the Hutus and Tutsis in Rwanda.

CHART AND GRAPH SKILLS
Compare Tables

Directions The tables below compare the populations, ethnic groups, dates of independence, and leaders for some countries in East and Southern Africa. Study the tables. Then answer the questions and complete the activities on the next page.

East Africa				
Country	**Population**	**Ethnic Groups**	**Date of Independence**	**Heads of State**
Djibouti	451,442	Afar, Arab, European, Somali	June 27, 1977	President and Prime Minister
Ethiopia	64,117,000	Afar, Amhara, Gurage, Oromo, Shankella, Sidamo, Somali, Tigre	Always Independent	President and Prime Minister
Uganda	23,317,560	Acholi, Arab, Asian, Baganda, Bagisu, Basogo, Batobo, Bunyoro, European, Karamojong, Langi, Lugbara, Rwanda	October 9, 1962	President
Somalia	7,253,137	Arab, Bantu, Somali	July 1, 1960	None

Southern Africa				
Country	**Population**	**Ethnic Groups**	**Date of Independence**	**Heads of State**
Botswana	1,576,470	Basarwa, Batswana, European, Kalanga, Kgalagadi	September 30, 1966	President
Lesotho	2,143,141	Asian, European, Sotho	October 4, 1966	King and President
Mozambique	19,104,696	Asian, Chokwe, European, Makua, Manyika, Shangaan, Sena	June 25, 1975	President and Prime Minister
Swaziland	1,083,289	European, Swazi, Shangaan, Tonga, Zulu	September 6, 1968	King and Prime Minister

(continued)

   Use after reading Chapter 14, Skill Lesson, pages 506–507.

Name ____ Date ___________________

1 Which of the countries in East and Southern Africa have kings?

Lesotho, Swaziland

2 Which East or Southern African country has always been an independent nation?

Ethiopia

3 Which East or Southern African country has the largest population? Which

country has the smallest? Ethiopia, Djibouti

4 Name the East and Southern African countries that have both Presidents and

Prime Ministers leading their people. Mozambique, Ethiopia, and Djibouti

5 Which Southern African countries have Shangaan people living within them?

Swaziland and Mozambique

6 Which countries have Europeans as part of their populations?

Djibouti, Lesotho, Mozambique, Swaziland, Botswana, and Uganda

7 Which East or Southern African nation has no head of state?

Somalia

8 The Baganda, Bagisu, and Basogo people live in which country?

Uganda

Directions Use the tables to help you order the following lists. Write the
numbers 1–4 on the lines next to each country.

9 Countries by population
(Highest to Lowest)

  4   Botswana

  3   Somalia

  2   Mozambique

  1   Uganda

10 Countries by Date of Independence
(First to Last)

  2   Lesotho

  4   Djibouti

  1   Uganda

  3   Swaziland

East and Southern Africa

 **Directions** Complete this graphic organizer to show that you understand how to use facts and details to make generalizations about East Africa and Southern Africa.

FACTS + DETAILS	→	GENERALIZATION

Many East and Southern African countries have weak economies. They must deal with ethnic conflicts, famine, disease, and large amounts of foreign debt. Also, protecting the environment is a major concern.

Students should mention that many East and Southern African countries have economic, health care, and environmental problems.

People from the many different world regions, including the Arabian peninsula and Europe, have settled in Africa. Each group brought with it new cultural ideas and influences, such as languages, religions, and customs.

Students should mention that the cultures of East and Southern Africa are very diverse because of the many groups that settled there.

      Use after reading Chapter 14, pages 476–509.

Name _________________________________ Date ____________

Test Preparation

Directions Read each question and choose the best answer. Then fill in the circle for the answer you have chosen. Be sure to fill in the circle completely.

1 The tall, steep cliffs that lie along Africa's east coast are called—
  Ⓐ rifts.
  Ⓑ grasslands.
  Ⓒ escarpments.
  Ⓓ pans.

2 The Afrikaaners are descendants of which people who settled in South Africa during the seventeenth century?
  Ⓕ Khoisan
  Ⓖ Portuguese
  Ⓗ English
  Ⓙ Dutch, French, and German

3 Why are many of the East African Lakes known as "Soda Lakes"?
  Ⓐ The lakes are full of salt water.
  Ⓑ The lakes are full of acid water.
  Ⓒ The lake water is neither fresh nor salt water, but alkaline.
  Ⓓ The lakes are drying up and losing water.

4 The South African policy of apartheid was designed to—
  Ⓕ keep people of European descent in control of the government and separate all the country's racial groups.
  Ⓖ establish a country of equal people regardless of race.
  Ⓗ keep the country as a British colony.
  Ⓙ recognize the African National Congress Party as a political party.

5 Many African nations are burdened with foreign debt. What is one solution that may solve the debt problem?
  Ⓐ The UN and other world organizations could stop lending money to African countries.
  Ⓑ The African countries could give foreign aid money to their leaders.
  Ⓒ The foreign debt could be canceled or repayment postponed.
  Ⓓ The UN could pay off the debt.

Use after reading Chapter 14, pages 476–509.

Great Rivers, Mighty Monsoons

Directions South Asia has many different landforms and bodies of water. Study the map of the region, and label each landform and body of water. Use the clues below and your textbook to help you complete the activity.

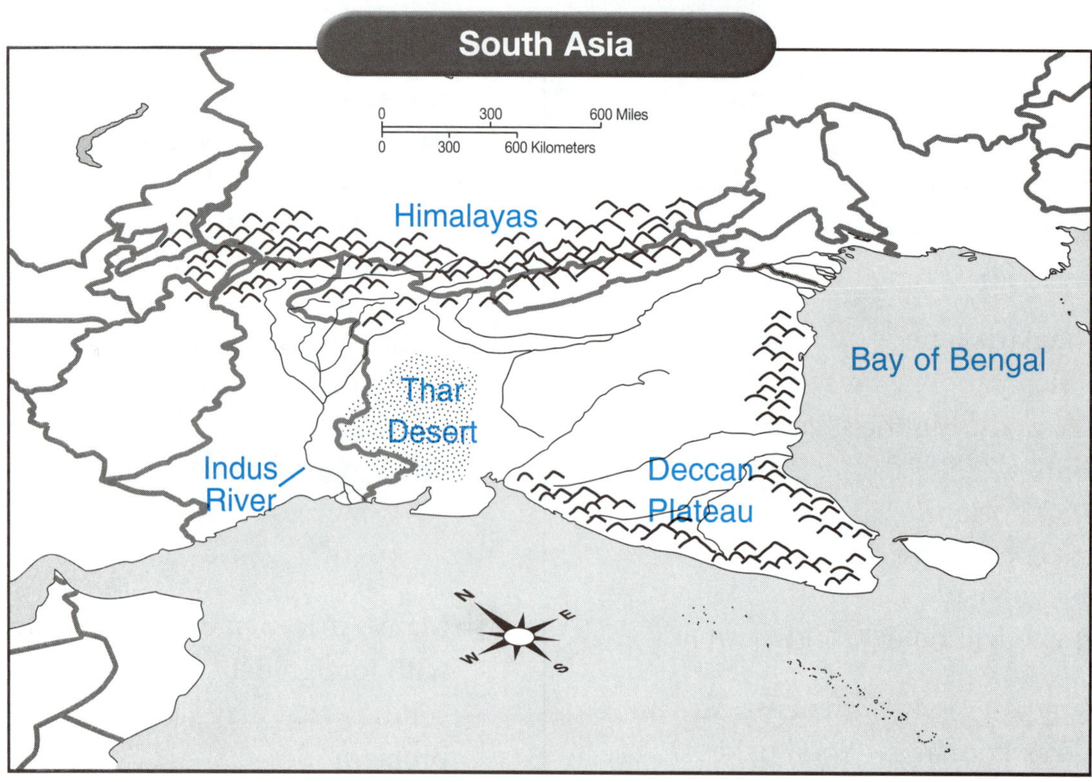

1 A massive mountain range with 95 peaks

the Himalayas

2 A body of water that is located along the eastern edge of the Indian subcontinent

Bay of Bengal

3 A high, flat area in the center of the Indian subcontinent; where most of the region's minerals are found

Deccan Plateau

4 A hot, dry region bordering the Ganges Plain and the Himalayas

Thar Desert

5 A large river and source of irrigation for the farmers of Pakistan

Indus River

Through the Ages

Directions Read the quotes below, which might have been said by South Asians at different times in history. Decide which group each speaker was talking about, select the name of that group from the box, and write it in the space provided. Use your textbook to help you complete the activity.

| Aryans | Moguls | People in Mohenjo-Daro | Mauryans | Arabs |

1 "They swept over the land from the north. They were nomads who had little use for our towns. Some of my people fled south. Some of us were captured and enslaved. Those of us who were captured were placed at the bottom of the social system. Nothing will ever be the same in the Indus Valley."

Aryans

2 "Like so many others before, these people came from the west and conquered Sind. These invaders saw our kingdoms at war and thought it was the best time to invade. They brought their religion with them. They call it Islam."

Arabs

3 "Our rulers are descendants of the great king Babur, who swept into India in 1526. Babur set up a beautiful capital city at Agra. Today our rulers are still descendants of Babur, but they take orders from the British. Our rulers always agree with them."

Moguls

4 "Our ruler Asoka is the third great king in the family. His father and grandfather both established our empire. At Perot, Asoka was ruthless. Now, however, he has embraced Buddhism."

Mauryans

5 "My people have set up a wonderful city on the Indus River. Our city has wide streets and clay-brick homes. My home has a bathroom and plumbing. Next door is a shop where bread is baked. Far to the north is another city, called Harappa. I hear it is similar to my great city."

People in Mohenjo-Daro

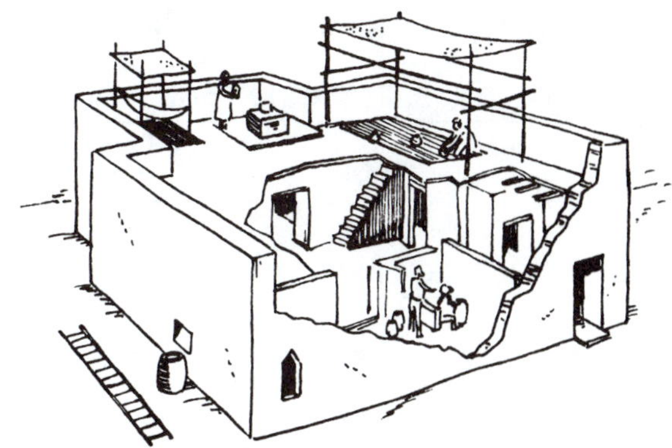

People and Culture

Directions Study the pictures of the different styles of clothing worn in the countries of India, Nepal, Pakistan, and Sri Lanka. Next to each picture, write the name of the country in which it is worn and a description of the clothing.

Shawar Kameez

Country:

Pakistan

Description:

A shawar kameez is worn by men and women.

It has baggy, pajama-like pants called the shawar

and a long tunic called the kameez.

Dupatta

Country:

Pakistan

Description:

A dupatta is a long scarf worn by Muslim women.

It is worn over the head, drapes across the chest,

and hangs down the back.

Sari

Country:

India, Sri Lanka, and other South Asian countries

Description:

A sari is a large piece of cloth worn by women.

One end covers the head or shoulder, and the

other end forms a long skirt.

READING SKILLS
Predict a Likely Outcome

Directions You can use what you know about the history of a place or an event to help you predict what might happen in the future. Read the paragraph about Bangladesh, and then complete the questions below.

Until the eighteenth century, Bangladesh had many different Muslim and Hindu rulers. In 1757 Bangladesh became part of the British Empire in India. For the next 190 years the people of Bangladesh and other groups in India pressed the British for independence. When the British decided to give India its independence in 1947, they created two countries based on religion—Hindu India and Muslim Pakistan. The area now known as Bangladesh, with its many Muslim people, became a part of Pakistan called East Pakistan. As a result, Pakistan was a divided nation with its two halves widely separated. Over the next few decades, many people in East Pakistan felt that they had little in common with those in the west. The Bangladeshi people saw the western Pakistanis as just another group of foreign rulers.

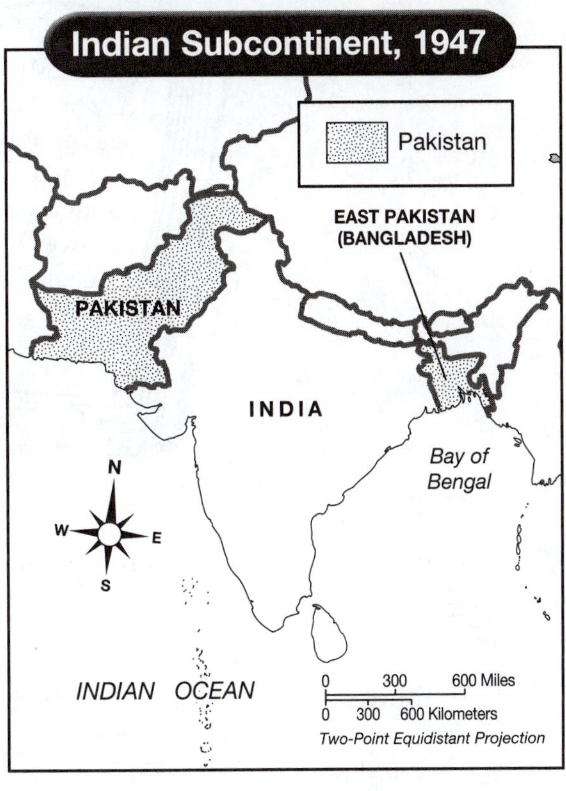

1 What did you learn about Bangladesh? The country had many rulers, including Muslims, Hindus, and the British. In 1947 Bangladesh became part of Pakistan, although it was separated from it by a great distance.

2 What do you think happened to Pakistan's rule over Bangladesh? Students will probably answer that Pakistan's rule ended in the years after 1947. The Bangladeshi people broke away from Pakistan and gained their independence in 1971.

South Asia Today

Directions Read this diary entry, which might have been written by a student traveling in India. Then write your own series of short entries about each of the places listed below. Make sure you include the ideas described next to the name of each place. Use your textbook and other resources to help you complete the activity.

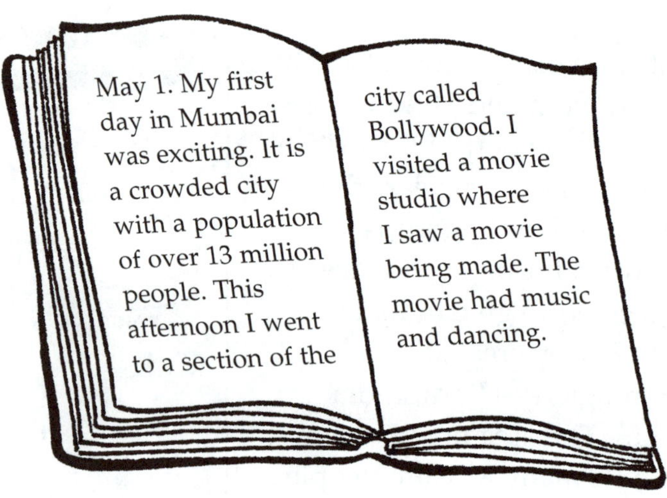

1 Mumbai; museums and other places to see

May 2:

Students' diary entries may vary. Entries should include details of visiting

museums, restaurants, and cafés.

2 A farming village; daily life of the people

May 6: Students' diary entries may vary.

Entries should include the daily work of men who tend to the fields or

livestock, and women who maintain the homes and families.

3 Kolkata; poverty and living conditions

May 8:

Students' diary entries may vary. Entries should include details of the mil-

lions of people in the city who are poor and without work or enough food.

      Use after reading Chapter 15, Lesson 4, pages 542–547.

CHART AND GRAPH SKILLS
Read a Population Pyramid

Directions Look at the population pyramids on this page. They show the populations of Bangladesh and Italy. Compare the population patterns of these countries, and then answer the questions on page 144.

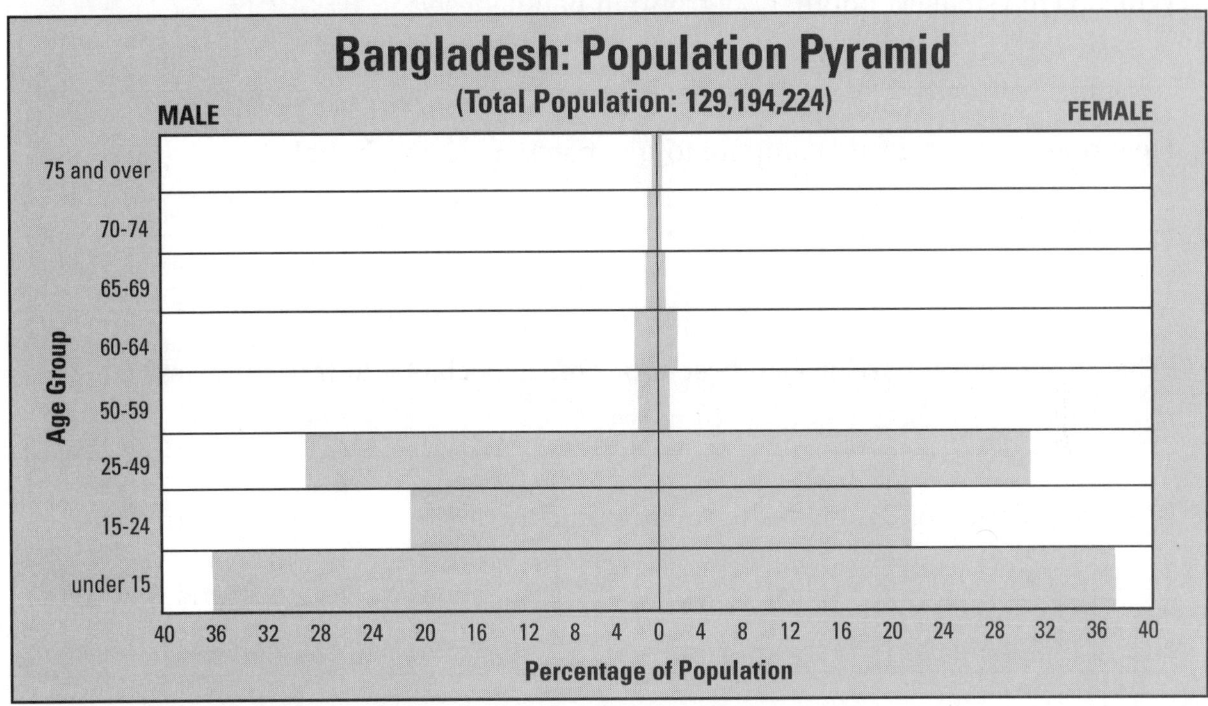

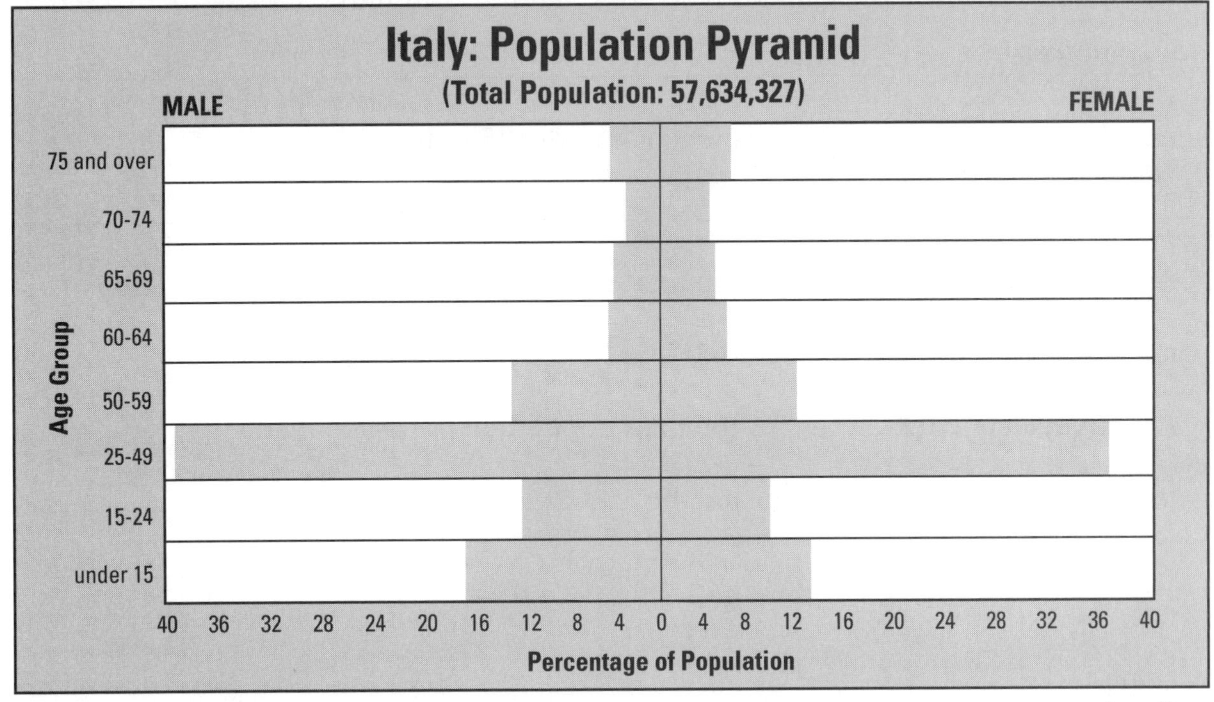

(continued)

1 Which is the largest population group in Bangladesh? under 15 years old

____

2 How does this age group compare to the matching group in Italy?

It is much larger.

3 Which is the smallest population group in Bangladesh? 75 and over

____

4 How does this age group compare to the matching group in Italy?

It is much smaller.

____

5 What do these comparisons suggest about life expectancy in the countries?

Italy has a higher life expectancy.

6 Is the population of Bangladesh growing quickly or slowly? How do you know?

Quickly. The largest population group in Bangladesh is under 15 years old, which

shows the population's quick growth.

7 Are there more males or females who are 75 and over in Italy?

females

8 Are there more males or females who are under 15 in Italy?

males

9 Approximately what percent of the total population of Bangladesh is made up of

males between the ages of 15 and 24? 22 percent

10 Approximately what percent of the total population of Italy is made up of

females between the ages of 25 and 49? 37 percent

South Asia

Directions Complete this graphic organizer to show that you understand how to write facts and opinions about South Asia.

TOPIC	FACT	OPINION
The Ganges River	Possible response: The Ganges River begins in the Himalayas.	Students should write an opinion about each topic. Accept all reasonable answers.
Sri Lanka	Possible response: Sri Lanka was formerly known as Ceylon.	
Mohandas Gandhi	Possible response: Gandhi became the leader of the Indian National Congress.	
Religions in South Asia	Possible response: South Asian religions include Islam, Hinduism, Buddhism, Christianity, and many others.	
India's Cities	Possible response: About 20 percent of India's people live in towns and cities.	
Clothing in South Asia	Students may mention the shawar kameez, chadder, or burka.	

15 Test Preparation

Name _______________________________   Date ___________

Directions Read each question and choose the best answer. Then fill in the circle for the answer you have chosen. Be sure to fill in the circle completely.

1 The flat farmland in southern Nepal is called the—
- Ⓐ Kathmandu.
- **Ⓑ** Terai.
- Ⓒ Mount Everest Region.
- Ⓓ Duars Plains.

2 Monsoons bring warm, moist air and heavy rains to the region. If the rains come from the Indian Ocean, then which month of the year is it?
- Ⓕ November
- Ⓖ January
- **Ⓗ** April
- Ⓙ December

3 A religion that does not worship a god or supreme being is—
- **Ⓐ** Jainism.
- Ⓑ Hinduism.
- Ⓒ Islam.
- Ⓓ Sikhism.

4 What is the name of the land that India and Pakistan continue to fight over?
- Ⓕ Nepal
- Ⓖ Sri Lanka
- **Ⓗ** Kashmir
- Ⓙ the Maldives

5 In which South Asian country is the literacy rate 90 percent of the population?
- Ⓐ Pakistan
- **Ⓑ** Sri Lanka
- Ⓒ Nepal
- Ⓓ India

Use after reading Chapter 15, pages 522–551.

Mountains, Deserts, Rivers, and Seas

Directions China can be described as a staircase with three separate steps.
The highest step refers to the land in western China. The lowest step refers to the
land along China's eastern coast. Read the list of physical and human features
below. Fill in the chart by writing the features on the correct "steps". Use your
textbook and the chart to help you answer the question that follows.

Features:

Plateau of Tibet	largest cities
source of the Huang He	coastline
source of the Chang Jiang	Northern Plateau
most productive farmland	Himalayas
largest population	source of the Xi River
Gobi (desert)	loess found in the Huang He

Steps:

West

- Himalayas
- Gobi (desert)
- source of the Chang Jiang
- source of the Huang He
- Plateau of Tibet

Central

- Northern Plateau
- loess found in the Huang He
- source of the Xi River

East

- coastline
- largest cities
- largest population
- most productive farmland

Why do you think most of the people in China live in the eastern part of the country?
Continue on another sheet of paper if necessary.

Answers will vary but should include some of the following: The climate is

milder there, so it is easier to live. The land and climate are also better for farming.

The seas and rivers provide transportation and make trade easier.

Long-Lasting Civilizations

Directions China has been the location of many empires—from the empire of the Shang Dynasty to the Manchus. Each empire had an effect on the culture and history of East Asia. Fill in the missing information about each of the Chinese ruling dynasties.

Shang Dynasty

• China's first dynasty

Zhou Dynasty

Possible response: established the Mandate of Heaven; adopted the

teachings of Confucius and Lao-tzu

Qin Dynasty

Possible response: gave China its name; united China under a strong

central government; standardized coins, weights, and writing; built the Great Wall

Han Dynasty

Possible response: set up universities, advanced mathematics, and developed

compasses; encouraged art and literature; traded with other parts of Asia and

Europe; conquered large areas of East Asia; spread Chinese culture to Japan and Korea

Mongols

• Traded goods such as silk, jewels, and porcelain with Marco Polo and Europe
• Controlled a vast empire that stretched to eastern Europe

Ming Dynasty

Possible response: isolated China from the world;

added thousands of miles onto the Great Wall

Qing Dynasty

• Established a peaceful empire
• Allowed much of China to fall under European influence

CHART AND GRAPH SKILLS
Read a Cartogram

Directions A population cartogram shows countries based on the number of people that live there. Countries with larger populations are shown larger than countries that have smaller populations. Study the population cartogram below. Then use it to complete the activities.

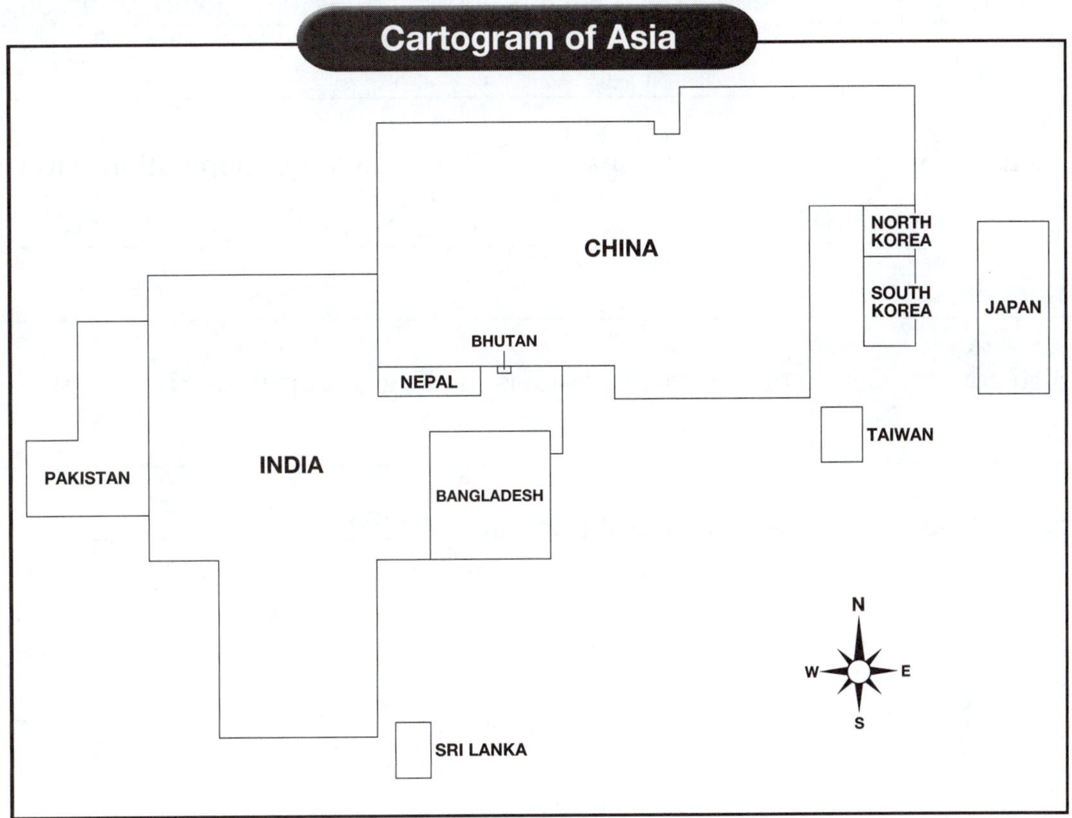

Directions Review the population cartogram above. Then order the following countries by population, starting with 1 for the country with the largest population.

_____5_____ North Korea 

_____6_____ Bhutan 

_____2_____ India 

_____1_____ China 

_____3_____ Pakistan 

_____4_____ Japan

(continued)

Directions Use the population cartogram on page 149 to answer the following questions about countries in East Asia.

1 Which country has a larger population, Bangladesh or South Korea?

Bangladesh

2 How can you tell which of the two nations has a larger population?

Bangladesh has more people because it is shown larger than South Korea on the

cartogram.

3 India has a larger land area than Japan. Does it have a larger population? How do

you know? Yes. India has a larger population, shown by its larger size on the

cartogram.

4 Which country shown on the cartogram has the largest population?

China

5 Which island country has the largest population? Japan

A Life of Traditions and Religions

Directions The teachings of Confucius are still popular around the world. Read the sayings of Confucius that are listed below. Then on the blank scroll, write your own Confucian saying about each of the topics. Share your sayings with the class.

Education

To eat your fill but not apply your mind to anything all day is a problem.

Good Manners

Good people bring out what is good in others, not what is bad.

Respect Others

Do not do to others what you would not want yourself.

Respect and Honor Parents

A young man's duty is to behave well to his parents at home and to his elders abroad.

Students' sayings may vary but should include the idea of the importance of education.

Students' sayings may vary but should include the idea that good manners and being polite are important.

Students' sayings may vary but should include the idea of treating others with respect.

Students' sayings may vary but should include the idea of treating parents and elders with respect.

A Region of Contrasts

Directions Read the statements about the economies of the East Asian countries. Decide if each statement is true or false. In the space provided, write *T* if it is true or *F* if it is false. Use your textbook if necessary.

1. __F__ China's economy is based on a system called keiretsu, in which companies maintain strong ties with each other.

2. __F__ South Korea exports minerals and metal products.

3. __T__ Japan has strengthened the economies of many other East Asian countries by investing in them.

4. __F__ The city of P'yongyang is a Special Economic Zone.

5. __T__ Japan is a country that imports raw materials to create products for export.

6. __T__ The economy of North Korea is far behind the economies of the rest of East Asia.

7. __T__ The city of Hong Kong is a Special Economic Zone.

8. __T__ China's Special Economic Zones are along its eastern coast.

East Asia

Directions Complete this graphic organizer to show that you understand how to draw conclusions about East Asia.

WHAT YOU READ 	WHAT YOU KNOW 	CONCLUSION
The Pacific Ocean provides the countries of East Asia with many benefits, such as fishing and routes for trading and transportation. However, monsoons bring heavy rains in the summer and strong winds in the winter. Parts of East Asia are on the Ring of Fire and are prone to volcanic eruptions, earthquakes, and tsunamis.	Students may mention that the Pacific Ocean provides many resources, but there is also a danger of monsoons, volcanoes, earthquakes, and tsunamis.	Students may mention that the people of East Asia benefit from the Pacific Ocean's resources, but there is also a danger of natural disasters.
Students should mention that Confucius was a Chinese teacher who stressed the importance of education, good manners, and respect for tradition.	**The ideas of philosophers and thinkers often have an influence on culture. Confucius had a lot of sayings people still refer to today. Religion plays an important part in the lives of many people around the world.**	Students may mention that the teachings of Confucius have influenced the culture of China and that they are still important to many people today.

Name _______________________   Date _______________

Test Preparation

Directions Read each question and choose the best answer. Then fill in the circle for the answer you have chosen. Be sure to fill in the circle completely.

1 Earth's tallest mountain range is called the—
- Ⓐ Taklimakan.
- **Ⓑ Himalayas.**
- Ⓒ Top of the World.
- Ⓓ Gobi.

2 The Japanese islands are—
- **Ⓕ the peaks of a long underwater mountain range.**
- Ⓖ made up of coral and sand.
- Ⓗ covered with flat farmlands.
- Ⓙ not affected by the winds that blow over the water.

3 The _______ Dynasty of China expanded the country's borders and spread Chinese culture to Korea and Japan.
- Ⓐ Qing
- **Ⓑ Han**
- Ⓒ Manchu
- Ⓓ Zhou

4 Which teaching or religion stressed a simple life in harmony with nature?
- Ⓕ Confucianism
- Ⓖ Shintoism
- **Ⓗ Daoism**
- Ⓙ Buddhism

5 Japan's economy is—
- **Ⓐ based on exporting high-quality manufactured products.**
- Ⓑ based on exporting minerals and fossil fuels.
- Ⓒ not successful compared to other countries in East Asia.
- Ⓓ a command economy.

Use after reading Chapter 16, pages 552–581.

Peninsulas, Islands, and Seas

Directions Be a cartographer. Create your own map of mainland Southeast Asia. First, study the map on page 585 of your textbook. Then answer the questions below. Next, draw the map in the space provided. Include on your map the answers to the questions.

1 What countries are located on the mainland of Southeast Asia?

Myanmar, Thailand, Cambodia, Vietnam, Laos, and Malaysia

2 What is the peninsula on which five of the mainland countries are located?

Indochina

3 What is the peninsula on which Malaysia and part of Thailand are located?

the Malay Peninsula

4 What river flows through Laos, Thailand, Cambodia, and southern Vietnam?

the Mekong River

5 Which strait and large sea separate the mainland of Southeast Asia from the island countries of the region? the Strait of Malacca and the South China Sea

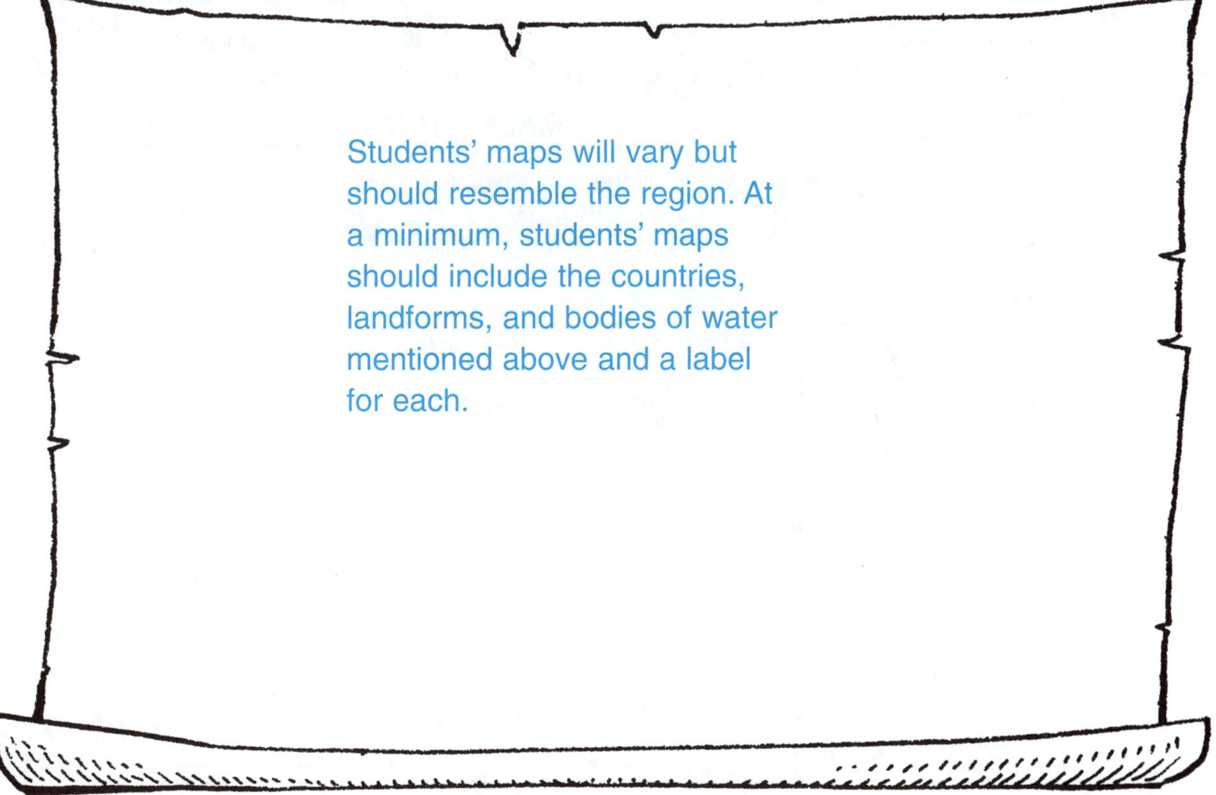

MAP AND GLOBE SKILLS
Compare Maps of Different Scale

Directions Map scales compare the distances on maps with the actual distances. Study these maps, and answer the questions that follow.

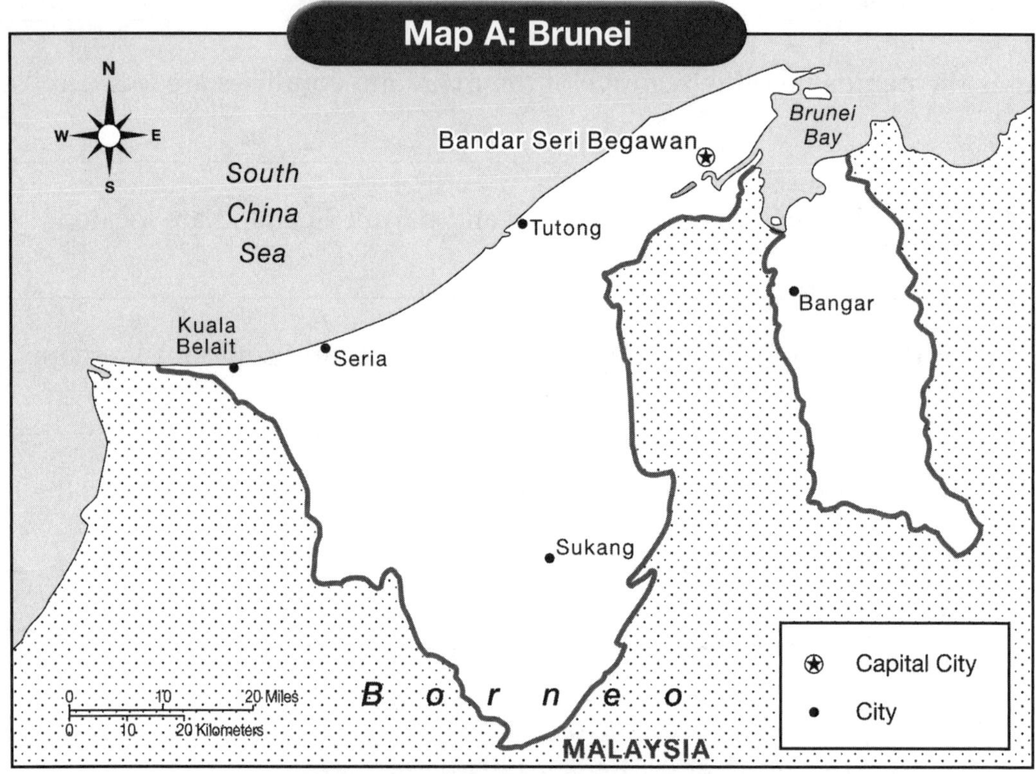

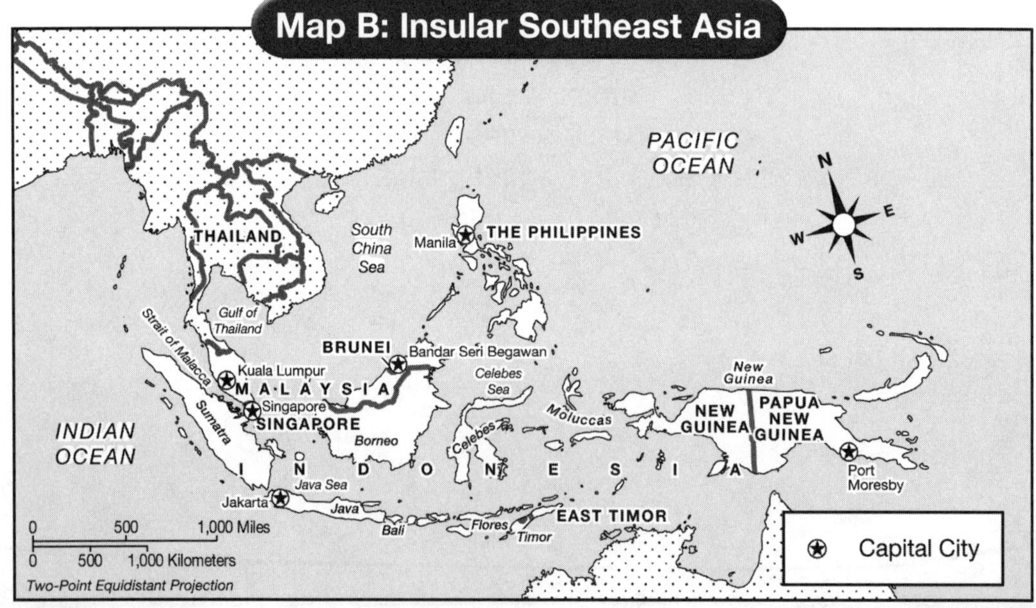

(continued)

Use after reading Chapter 17, Skill Lesson, pages 590–591.

Name ____ Date ________________

1 Which map shows the country of Brunei in more detail? Map A: Brunei

2 Which map would you use to find the distance between the cities of Jakarta and

Bandar Seri Begawan? Map B: Insular Southeast Asia

3 In which country is the city of Tutong located? Brunei

4 On which map did you find the city of Tutong? Explain why you chose that map.

Map A: Brunei. The map has a larger scale than Map B and shows more detail

of Brunei, making it easier to find the cities in that country.

5 Which map shows a larger area of Southeast Asia? Why? Map B: Insular Southeast

Asia. The map shows a larger land area because it has a smaller scale.

Directions Study the scales of the two maps on page 156, then answer the questions below.

6 Which city is farther from Manila—Jakarta or Port Moresby?

Port Moresby

7 How many miles apart are the cities Bandar Seri Begawan and Tutong?

approximately 20 miles

8 How many miles apart are the cities Singapore and Jakarta?

approximately 500 miles

9 How far apart are the two parts of Malaysia? approximately 400 miles

10 Which islands are closer to each other—the islands Java and Timor or the islands

New Guinea and Borneo? Java and Timor are closer to each other than are

New Guinea and Borneo.

In the Shadow of Others

Directions An outline is a list of important ideas that organize information about a topic. An outline shows you how important ideas relate to one another. The history of Southeast Asia is a large topic. Study the outline below of the region's history. Use your textbook to help you fill in the missing information.

I. Early Cultures and Kingdoms
   A. Different Ethnic Groups

      1. People from China migrated south to the region.

      2. The early settlers developed into many different ethnic groups, including the Mons, Khmers, and Malays.

   B. Early Kingdoms

      1. The Mons established the Kingdom of Funan in the first century A.D.

      2. Around A.D. 800 the Khmers established a Hindu Kingdom called Angkor-Khmer.

      3. The Malay people of Sumatra established a Buddhist kingdom called Srivijaya that lasted until A.D. 1290.

II. New Arrivals to the Region
   A. New Ethnic Groups and Religions

      1. Thai people arrived in the 1200s and began to establish powerful kingdoms.

      2. Arab traders and settlers introduced Islam to the region.

   B. The Europeans Arrive

      1. Starting in the 1500s, Portuguese, Dutch, Spanish, and English traders arrived.

      2. The Europeans took control of the entire region.

III. World War II to Present
   A. World War II and Independence

      1. The Japanese conquered all of Southeast Asia during World War II.

      2. After World War II, many countries in the region began to win independence from the Europeans.

      3. Communist and non-communist groups struggled for power in many countries.

Varying Economies, Varying Governments

Directions Both Brunei and Thailand have governments with monarchs.
Compare these governments by studying the charts below. Then complete
the statements below, underlining the correct term.

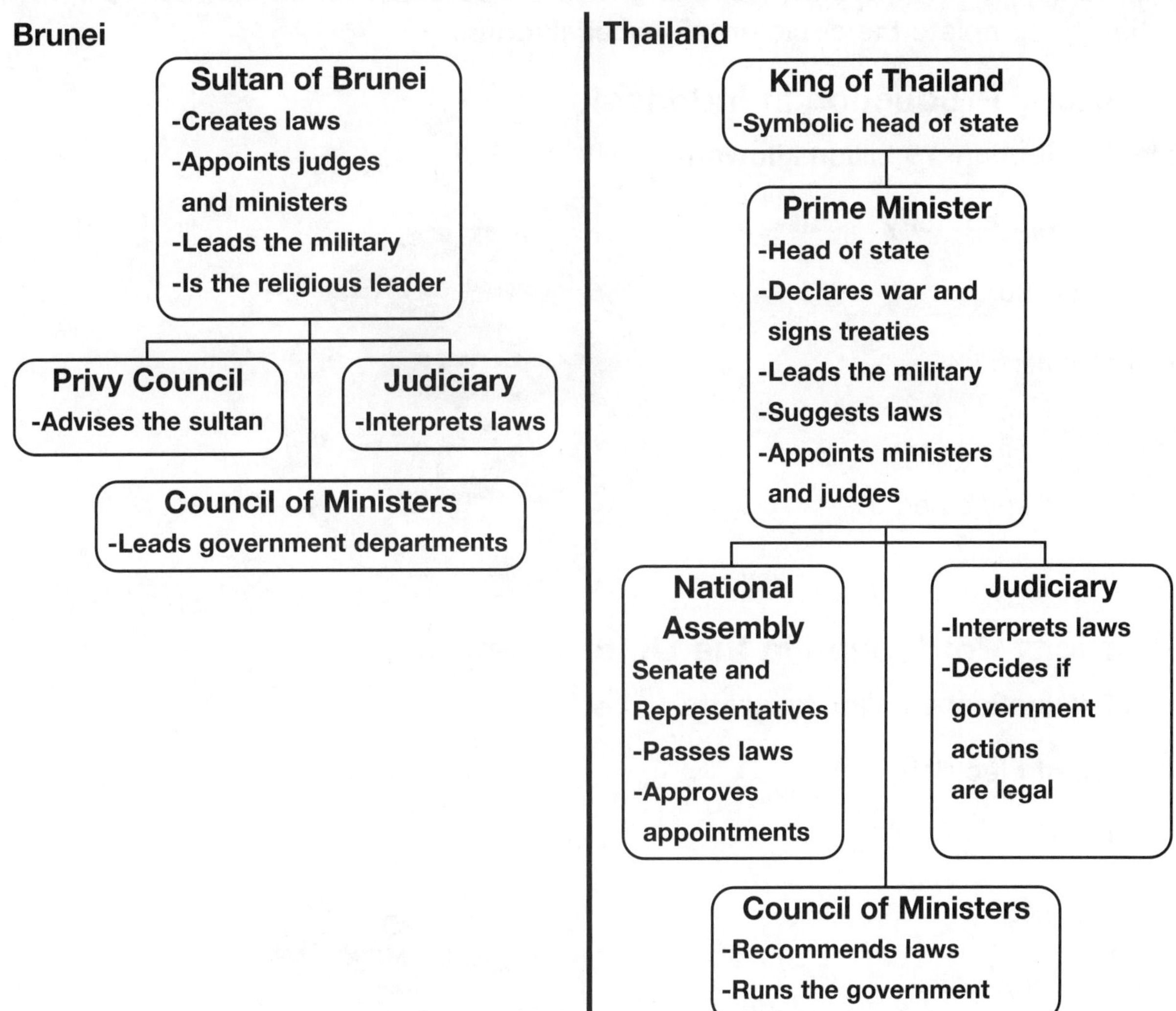

1 In Brunei the (**sultan**/Privy Council) is the head of state.

2 In Thailand the (National Assembly/**king**) and the (**prime minister**/Council of Ministers) are the heads of state.

3 In Thailand the (Council of Ministers/**National Assembly**) passes laws.

4 In Brunei, laws are created by the (**sultan**/Council of Ministers).

5 In both countries the (**Judiciary**/National Assembly) interprets laws.

CHART AND GRAPH SKILLS
Compare Circle Graphs

Directions Electricity is an important form of energy in Southeast Asia as well as in the United States. Listed below are the sources of electricity in both Indonesia and the United States, along with the percents for each. Use the information to complete the circle graph for each country.

Electricity Production in Indonesia

Total Production: 79 billion kilowatts

Sources of Electricity:

fossil fuels: 80%

hydroelectric: 15%

nuclear energy: 0%

wind, solar, and other: 5%

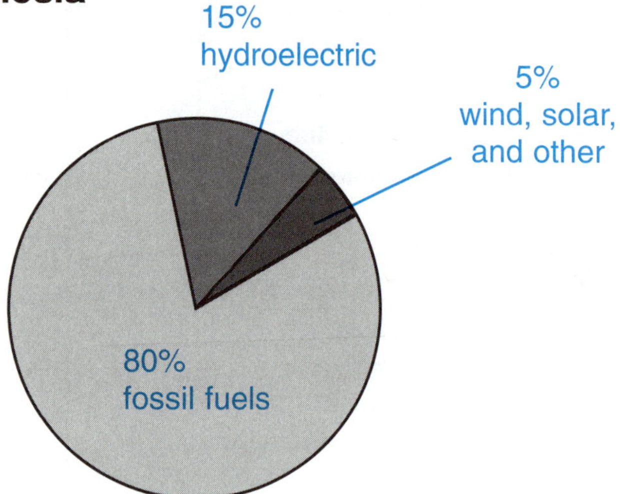

Electricity Production in the United States

Total Production: 4 trillion kilowatts

Sources of Electricity:

fossil fuels: 70%

hydroelectric: 8%

nuclear energy: 20%

wind, solar, and other: 2%

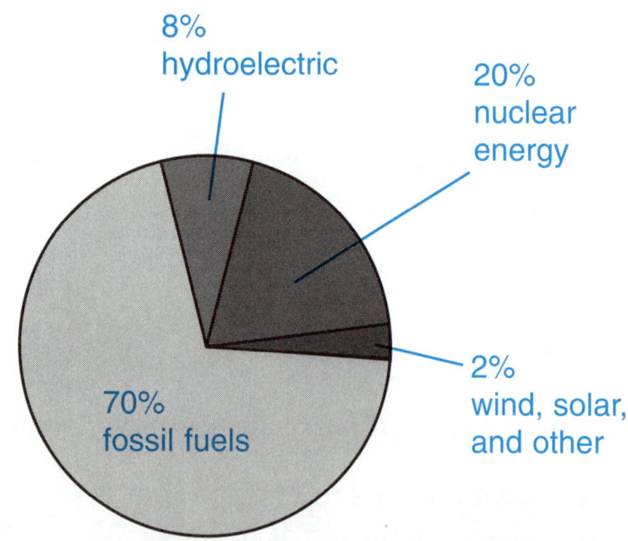

(continued)

     Use after reading Chapter 17, Skill Lesson, pages 602–603.

Name ____ Date _______________________

1 Which country produces more kilowatts of electricity? the United States _______________

2 How many general sources of electricity does Indonesia have? Name the sources.

three; fossil fuels, hydroelectric sources, and wind, solar and other sources

____

3 Which source of electricity is found in the United States but not in Indonesia?

nuclear energy

4 What is the largest source used to produce electricity in the United States?

fossil fuels

5 Three general sources of electricity are used in both Indonesia and the United States. Which of these three sources generates the smallest amount of electricity?

wind, solar, and other sources

6 What is the largest source used to produce electricity in Indonesia?

fossil fuels

7 Compare the percentages of electricity generated from hydroelectric sources in both countries. How much more electricity is generated in Indonesia from this source than

in the United States? 7%

8 Which general energy source produces 5% of Indonesia's supply of electricity?

wind, solar, and other sources

9 Which do you think is easier to read, the list of sources of electricity or the circle graph?

Explain. Responses will vary: many students may comment that the information

is easier to read in the form of a circle graph.

Southeast Asia

Directions Complete this graphic organizer to show that you understand cause-and-effect relationships about Southeast Asia.

CAUSE		EFFECT

Students should indicate that many rain forests have been cut down in Southeast Asia. → Many kinds of animals are now considered endangered or threatened in Southeast Asia.

Plates on Earth's surface in Southeast Asia continue to shift. → Students should indicate that Southeast Asia has earthquakes and volcanoes.

Students should indicate that Laos is landlocked. → Laos has difficulty trading with countries other than its neighbors.

Past wars and political problems plague Vietnam. → Students should indicate that Vietnam is still a communist state.

Name ______________________   Date __________

Test Preparation

Directions Read each question and choose the best answer. Then fill in the circle for the answer you have chosen. Be sure to fill in the circle completely.

1 A part of Southeast Asia made up of many islands is—
- Ⓐ Mainland Southeast Asia.
- Ⓑ Laos.
- **Ⓒ Insular Southeast Asia.**
- Ⓓ Isthmus of Kra.

2 The weather in Southeast Asia is almost always—
- Ⓕ neither hot nor cool.
- Ⓖ dry and hot.
- Ⓗ dry and cool.
- **Ⓙ hot and humid.**

3 The _______ Kingdom of Srivijaya took control of the trade that flowed between India and China.
- **Ⓐ Malay**
- Ⓑ Chinese
- Ⓒ Khmer
- Ⓓ Mon

4 The idea that country after country would be taken over by communists was known as the—
- Ⓕ protectorate.
- **Ⓖ domino effect.**
- Ⓗ East Indies effect.
- Ⓙ Southeast Asia plan

5 Which nation has a strong economy based mostly on the technology and banking industries but has almost no agriculture?
- Ⓐ Thailand
- Ⓑ Indonesia
- Ⓒ the Philippines
- **Ⓓ Singapore**

The Lands Down Under

Directions Australia and New Zealand have diverse climates, landforms, animals, and plant life. Compare the two countries by completing the chart. Fill in the boxes for each category with specific names or details. Use your textbook to help you complete the activity.

Australia

New Zealand

— Climate —

Answers may include: tropical along the northern coast, hot and dry in central and western regions, southeast and southwest coasts receive year-round rain.

Answers may include: warm summers, cold winters, and year-round rain.

— Landforms —

Answers may include: Great Dividing Range, Murray and Darling Rivers, grasslands, a western plateau, deserts, the Uluru Rock, and the Great Barrier Reef.

Answers may include: the Southern Alps, the North Island and South Island, foothills, plains, volcanoes, geysers, rivers, waterfalls, and many lakes.

— Animals —

Answers may include: kangaroo, koala bear, duckbilled platypus, emu, kookaburra, sheep, and cattle.

Answers may include: kiwi birds, bats, reptiles, and sheep.

— Plants —

Answers may include: acacia and eucalyptus trees.

Answers may include: evergreen and deciduous trees.

Use after reading Chapter 18, Lesson 1, pages 620–624.

Outposts in the Pacific

Directions The Aborigines of Australia and the Maori of New Zealand were the first inhabitants of these lands. Read the list of activities below. Then make a check mark to show which group might have performed each one.

	Aborigines	The Maori
1 Weave clothing from flax.	☐	☑
2 Tell dreamtime stories.	☑	☐
3 Make rock art.	☑	☐
4 Hunt birds, seals, and whales.	☐	☑
5 Make tools from rocks and wood.	☐	☑
6 Ask a neighboring tribe for permission to hunt on their land.	☑	☐
7 Carve a boomerang from a tree branch.	☑	☐
8 Build a large wooden canoe.	☐	☑
9 Move with the family to a different location in search of food.	☑	☐
10 Speak with wise tribal elders.	☑	☐

Directions Imagine you are a member of one of the groups above. Write about what a day in your life would be like.

Responses will vary but should include some of the information from the checklist above.

____

____

____

____

____

CITIZENSHIP SKILLS

Act as a Responsible Citizen

Read about the problems Australians have with dingoes. Then state the problem and check off solutions that you think a responsible citizen might suggest. Make sure the solutions benefit the entire community.

Dingoes are wild dogs that first appeared in Australia thousands of years ago with Asian traders. The dogs spread quickly over the continent, hunting small mammals, reptiles, and birds. When the Europeans arrived, their sheep herds became another source of food for the dingoes. In 1960 the ranchers convinced the Australian government to build a fence to stop the dingoes from attacking their sheep. The fence stretches 3,307 miles from the state of South Australia to Queensland. Today the dingoes inside the fence are hunted by ranchers who want to protect their sheep. The dingoes on the outside of the fence live in barren lands with few sources of food. Some Australians are worried that the dingoes will be hunted or starved into extinction. They are also concerned that the populations of many other animals, such as the emu, are growing too large without the dingoes to keep them under control. Despite these protests the sheep ranchers and many other Australians are firm about keeping the dingoes outside the fence and want to continue hunting the dingoes that threaten their herds.

The Problem

Because dingoes kill sheep, sheep ranchers convinced the government to build a fence to stop the dingoes, and today the ranchers hunt dingoes. Some people fear the dingoes will become extinct and that the populations of the dingoes' natural prey will get out of control.

1 Inside the fenced area, set aside tracts of land where the dingoes can live and hunt the other animal species. ☑

2 Stop hunting the dingoes and push all of them outside the fence. ☐

3 Feed the dingoes on both sides of the fence and protect the sheep herds. ☑

4 Allow the dingoes to feed on the sheep herds. ☐

5 Continue pushing the dingoes outside the fence and hunting those found inside near the sheep herds. ☐

                    Use after reading Chapter 18, Skill Lesson, pages 632–633.

Australia and New Zealand Today

Directions Settlers in Australia introduced many new animals to the continent. Some had a devastating effect on the native plants and animals. Study the chart below that lists some of these animals and the effects they had on the continent. Then read each pair of statements. For each pair, place an X next to the statement that is supported by the information on the chart.

Animal	Reasons for Introduction	Results
Cat	• Pets • Control rodent population	• Destroy native rodents
Camel	• Desert transportation	• Form large wild herds
Cane toad	• Control insect population	• Multiply into large numbers • Become pests
Rabbit	• Sport hunting • Food	• Dig burrows that destroy vegetation and speed up desertification
Red fox	• Sport hunting • Control rabbit population	• Destroy rabbits and native marsupials

1 _______ Some animals were introduced to fill the barren land.

___X___ Some animals were introduced to correct the problems that were caused by other animals.

2 _______ Rabbits were introduced to control insects.

___X___ Rabbits were a source of food.

3 ___X___ The red fox was introduced for sport.

_______ The red fox was a solution to the cane toad problem.

4 _______ Cane toads and cats were introduced as pets.

___X___ Cats were introduced as pets.

5 ___X___ Camels carried products and passengers across the barren outback.

_______ Camels are still a main source of transportation.

CHART AND GRAPH SKILLS
Compare Line Graphs

Directions Read the paragraph below and study the line graphs. Then use the graphs to complete the activity on page 169.

Imagine you are working for Australia's Census Bureau. The line graphs below show you some information about a fictional Australian town named Oolamago. The town's population has doubled several times since the year 1900. The first shows the growth of the town's native population between the years 1900 and 2000. The next is a double-line graph. It shows the town's population of people from other countries and from other parts of Australia.

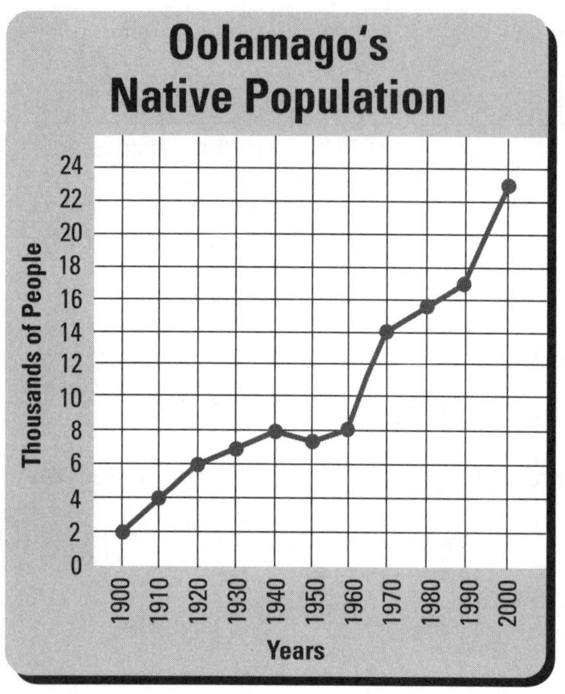

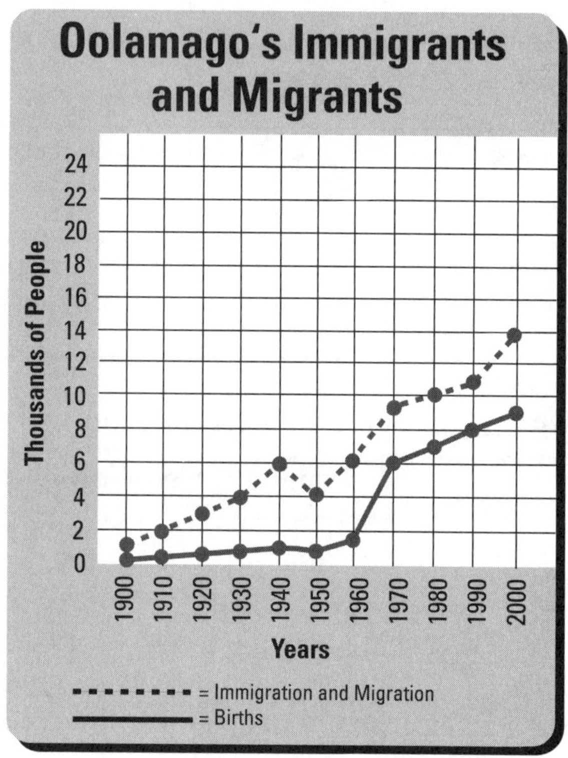

(continued)

   Use after reading Chapter 18, Skill Lesson, pages 640–641.

Directions The Census Bureau Chief has asked you to write a brief report analyzing Oolamago's population growth over the past century. Study the graphs on page 168. Then write your analysis following the outline below. Use a separate sheet of paper if you need more space.

I. Oolamago's Native Population from 1900–2000

    A. Growth between 1900 and 1940

    B. Decline between 1940 and 1950

    C. Rapid growth between 1960 and 1970

II. **Oolamago's Sources of Population Growth**

    A. Immigration

    B. Migration

Students' essays may vary, but should follow the outlined format above. For the overall population, students should report the continuous growth in population between 1900 and 1940. The essay should report the decline in growth during the World War II years and the period of rapid growth between 1960 and 1970. Students should discuss the sources of population growth and may note that the graphs show as much influence on population growth from immigration and migration as from births.

Australia and New Zealand

Directions Complete this graphic organizer to show that you can use your knowledge about European settlement to make inferences about culture in Australia and New Zealand today.

DETAILS + KNOWLEDGE  **INFERENCE**

DETAILS

People from Southeast Asia settled in Australia. They became known as Aborigines. They had no formal government, and they believed in dreamtime spirits. In New Zealand the first people came from Polynesia and called themselves the Maori. They formed tribes and honored gods of nature and their ancestors. Unlike the Aborigines, they were fierce warriors. In 1788 Britain began using Australia as a penal colony. Eventually, British colonists settled in Australia and New Zealand. Immigrants from around the world have also come to Australia and New Zealand.

KNOWLEDGE

Students should indicate a knowledge of European colonial settlements: Europeans changed the way that native peoples lived in many places; Europeans instituted their own forms of government; cultures of native peoples generally blended with those of other cultures. Accept all reasonable answers.

INFERENCE

Students should mention that European, Pacific, and Aboriginal cultures influenced Australia and New Zealand.

     Use after reading Chapter 18, pages 618–643.

18 Test Preparation

Directions Read each question and choose the best answer. Then fill in the circle for the answer you have chosen. Be sure to fill in the circle completely.

1 The Murray and Darling Rivers flow through which Australian landform?
- Ⓐ the grasslands
- Ⓑ the outback
- Ⓒ the western plateau
- Ⓓ Pacific Ocean coast

2 Much of the world's ______ comes from northeastern Australia and is used to make aluminum.
- Ⓕ iron
- Ⓖ copper
- Ⓗ bauxite
- Ⓙ nickel

3 The first settlers of New Zealand are called the Maori. The name *Maori* means—
- Ⓐ "ancient ancestors."
- Ⓑ "Polynesian."
- Ⓒ "local people."
- Ⓓ "island settlers."

4 One of the most important and fastest growing industries in Australia and New Zealand is—
- Ⓕ sheep ranching.
- Ⓖ tourism.
- Ⓗ gold mining.
- Ⓙ lumbering.

5 What happened in 1972 that forced Australia and New Zealand to build stronger economic ties with each other?
- Ⓐ Asia wanted to develop trade with Australia.
- Ⓑ The United States increased its influence in the South Pacific.
- Ⓒ New Zealand's population increased.
- Ⓓ Britain joined the European Economic Community.

Island Migrations

Directions The islands of the Pacific can be classified into three regions—Melanesia, Micronesia, and Polynesia. Thousands of years ago cultures spread as people moved from island to island. Trace the routes of these people on the map below by following the instructions on page 173.

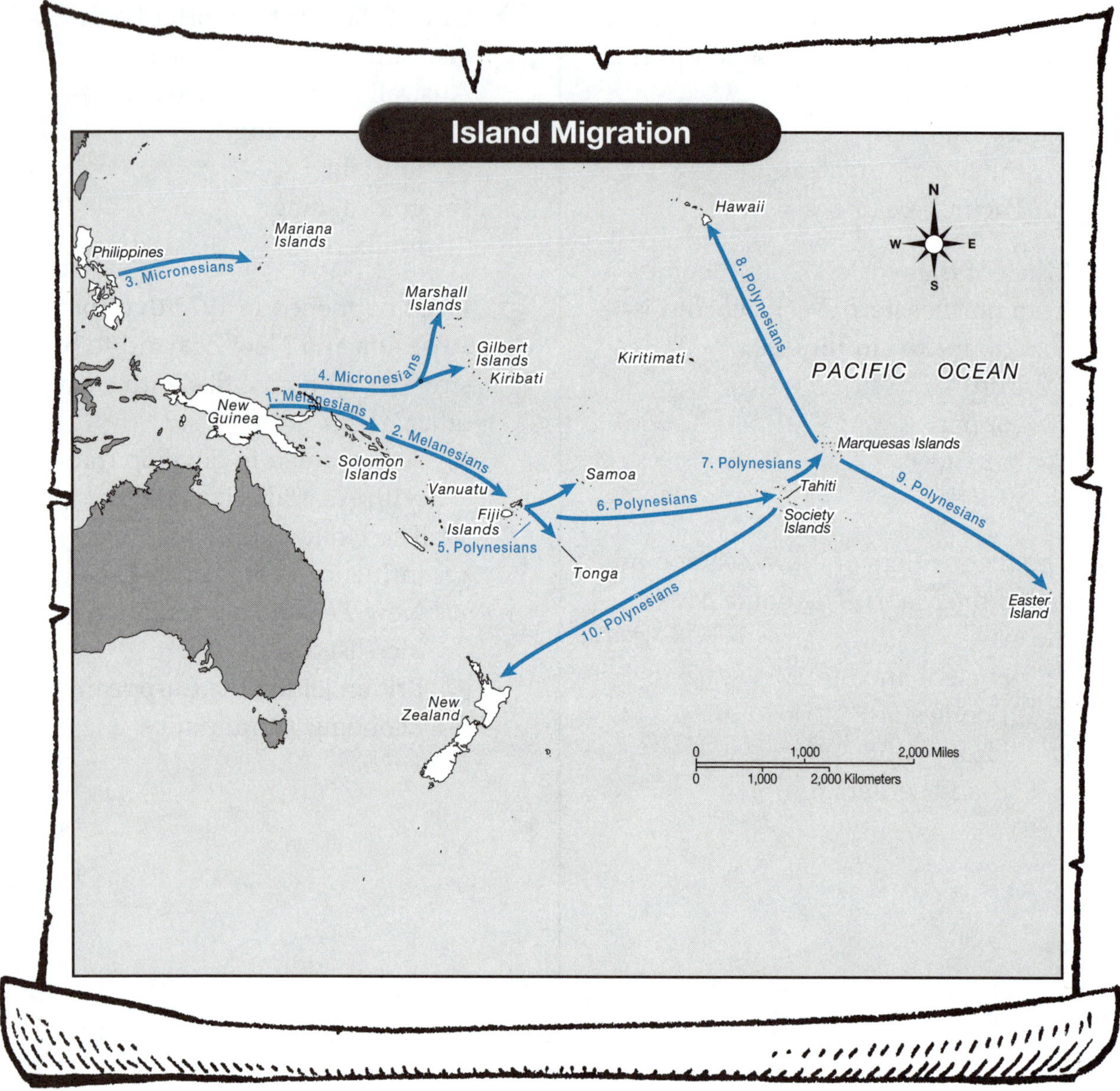

(continued)

Name ____ Date _________________

Directions **Read the following statements about migration patterns. Then draw arrows between the islands on the map to show each pattern. On each arrow, write the number of the corresponding statement and the name of the group.**

Melanesians

1 Melanesian people moved from New Guinea to the Solomon Islands.

2 From the Solomon Islands, the Melanesians migrated to Vanuatu and the Fiji Islands.

Micronesians

3 People from the Philippines settled the Mariana Islands.

4 Micronesian people from New Guinea and the Solomon Islands sailed east and north to the Gilbert and Marshall Islands.

Polynesians

5 Polynesian people from the Fiji Islands moved to Tonga and Samoa.

6 From Tonga and Samoa, the Polynesians settled Tahiti and the Society Islands.

7 These Polynesians settled the Marquesas Islands to the northeast.

8 Polynesians migrated from the Marquesas Islands north to Hawaii.

9 Polynesians from the Marquesas Islands settled Easter Island.

10 Polynesians from the Marquesas Islands moved southwest to New Zealand.

Study the map. Which group settled the largest area of the Pacific Ocean? What effect do you think the group's migration had on the region?

Students should identify the Polynesian group as the settlers of the largest area of the

Pacific region. Students' answers may vary but should include how the Polynesian

people of the region shared a similar way of life, including clans, languages,

and customs that spread as they settled on new islands.

Island Nations

Directions There are different kinds of islands in the Pacific Ocean. Study the pictures of two types below. Use your textbook to help you identify the island types, and write their names on the lines provided. Then answer the questions that follow.

 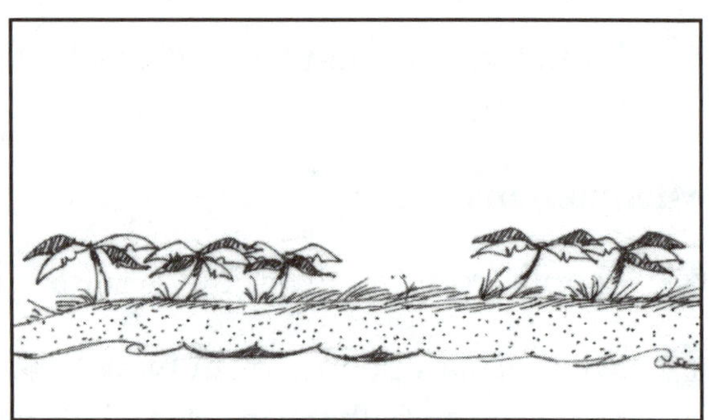

1 high island _______________________   **2** low island _______________________

3 Which kind of island was formed by an eruption that pushed a volcano above the water? the high island _______________________

4 Which kind of island was formed by thousands of small animals called coral that attached themselves to a small piece of land? the low island _______________________

5 Which kind of island has rich and fertile soils that can be used for agriculture?
the high island _______________________

6 Which kind of island is more likely to have dense forests of beech and pine trees?
the high island _______________________

7 Are forests more likely to grow on the eastern or western side of the islands' mountains? on the eastern side _______________________

8 On which kind of island are palm trees found? Both the high and low islands have palm trees. _______________________

9 Which kind of island is more likely to be inhabited and why?
The high island is more likely to be inhabited; it has more rainfall, more vegetation, and better soil.

     Use after reading Chapter 19, Lesson 2, pages 654–659.

MAP AND GLOBE SKILLS
Compare Different Kinds of Maps

Directions There are many kinds of maps. Each kind shows different information. It is important to learn how to read different maps and to relate them to each other. Study the maps below and on page 176 and use them to complete the activities that follow.

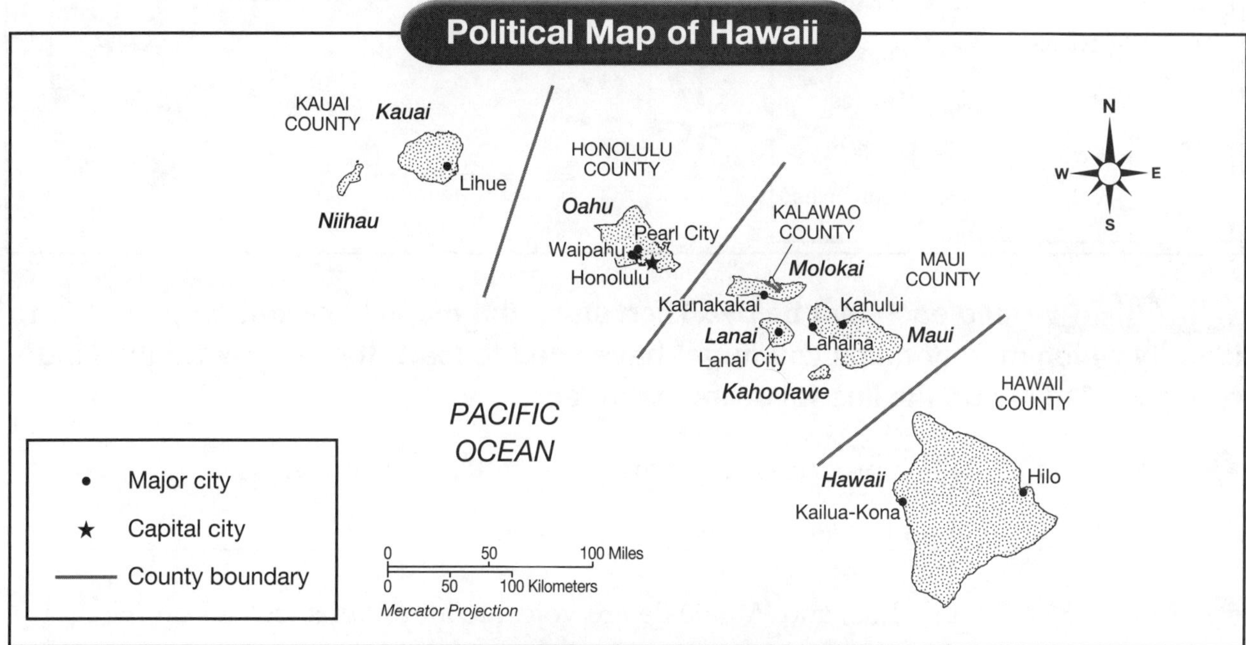

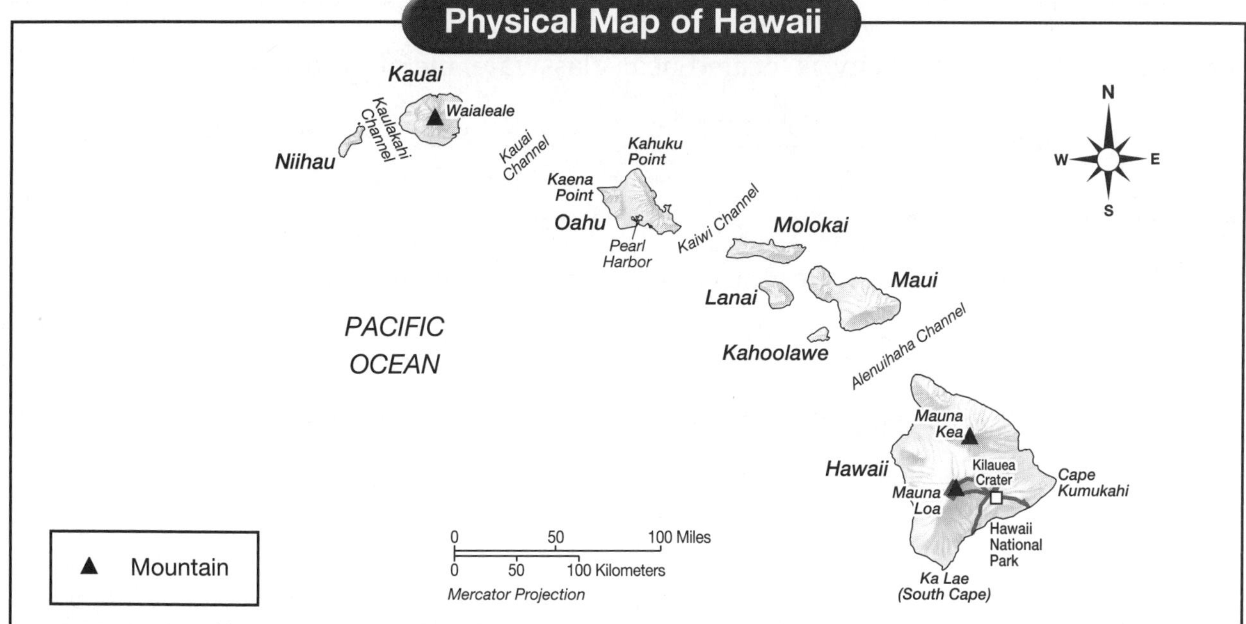

(continued)

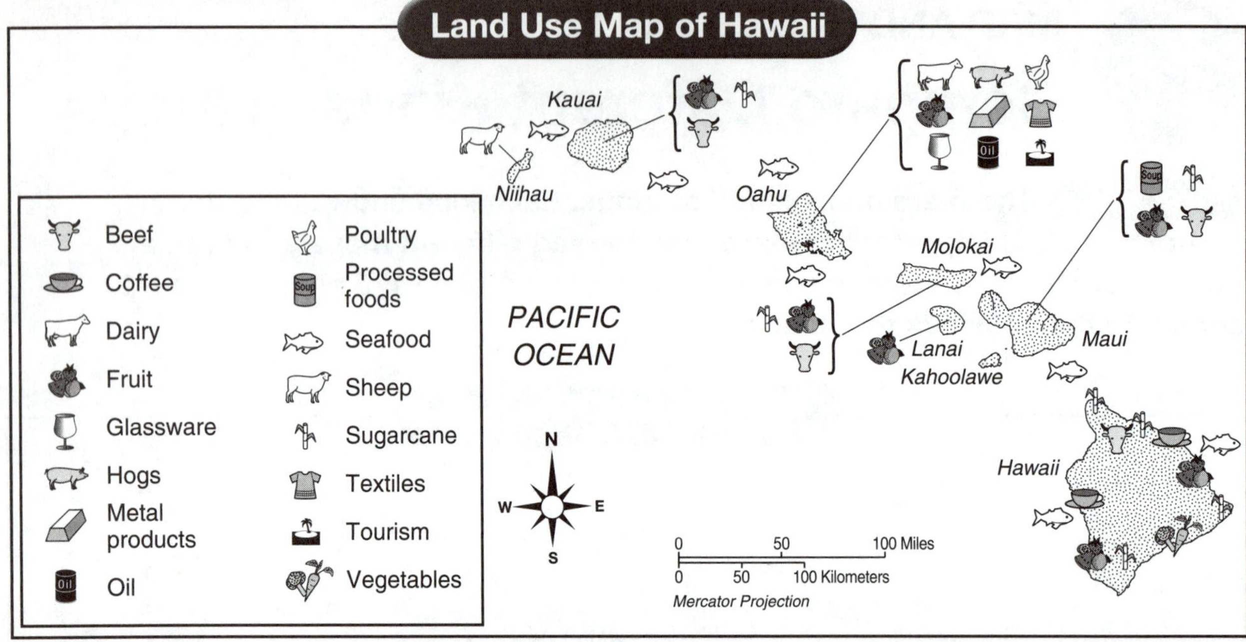

Directions Read each fact below. Then study the maps here and on page 175 to identify which map or maps you might have used to learn the fact. Write the kind or kinds of maps on the line following each fact.

1 The island of Hawaii produces sugarcane, beef cattle, and coffee.

the land use map of Hawaii

2 Mauna Kea, Mauna Loa, and Waialeale are volcanic mountains located on the islands of Hawaii and Kauai. the physical map of Hawaii

3 Honolulu, the capital city, is located near glassware, metal products, and textile industries. the political map of Hawaii and the land use map of Hawaii

4 The Kauai Channel separates the counties of Honolulu and Kauai.

the physical map of Hawaii and the political map of Hawaii

5 Hawaii's coffee industry is located around Mauna Loa and Mauna Kea.

the physical map of Hawaii and the land use map of Hawaii

     Use after reading Chapter 19, Skill Lesson, pages 660–661.

Antarctica: A Continent Without a Population

Directions Antarctica is a land without a permanent population, but humans do visit the frozen continent. Many scientists and tourists go there to study the barren land. A tourist visiting Antarctica may have written the following letters. Read the letters and write one more, about the rest of the tourist's visit. You may want to use your textbook or other resource materials to provide details for your letter.

November 1

Dear Mom and Dad,

We just landed on Antarctica's Ross Island at McMurdo, one of three United States research bases. The base is much larger than I expected. It has an airport, fuel depots, dormitories, and even a library. Many people stop here on their way to the South Pole. It is very cold here. Someone told me that the average temperature is ⁻56°F, and I believe it. I am wearing many layers of clothes, heavy boots, and a parka. The sun is bright because of the glare that reflects off the snow. To protect my eyes, I am wearing goggles. The people at the base drive around in special vehicles that have tracks instead of tires. The tracks stop the vehicle from sliding, but they also make it move slowly. Today I am going for a ride to explore the area outside the base. I will write again soon.

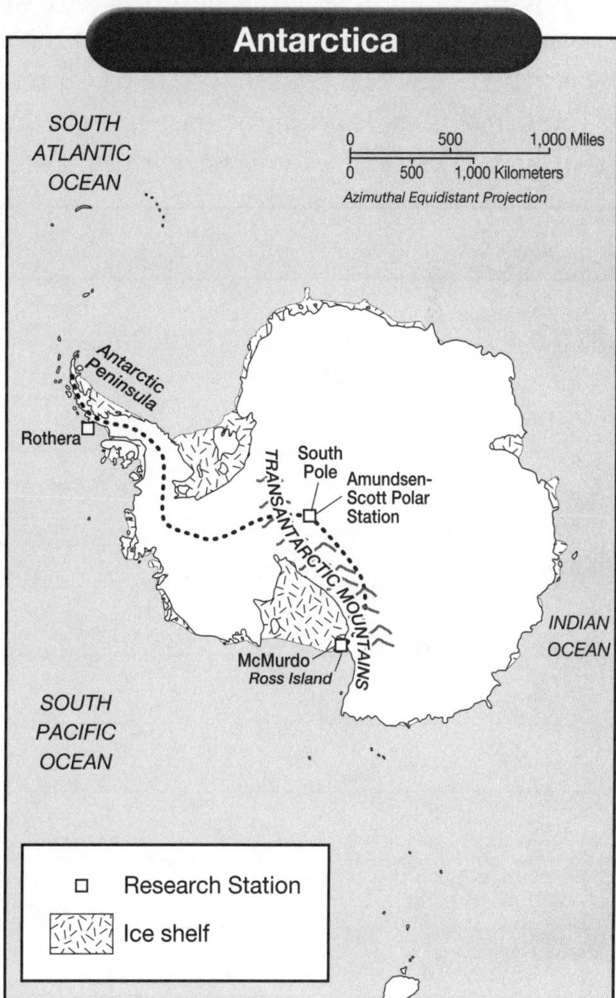

(continued)

November 6

Dear Mom and Dad,

I made it to the South Pole! I flew to the Amundsen-Scott Polar Station, the American base at the South Pole. The base is inside a giant dome that keeps everyone warm. I rushed right out to see two of the South Poles. That's right, there's more than one! One is the True Geographic South Pole, which is marked by a simple sign. Another is the Ceremonial South Pole. The Ceremonial South Pole is a short marker surrounded by flags from many countries. The flags are from the United States, the United Kingdom, Norway, and nine other countries. One of the scientists told me that every year they have to move the sign for the True Geographic South Pole. This is because every year the ice we are on slides about 30 feet over the land beneath it. Tomorrow I am leaving the base to visit the Transantarctic Mountains and then the Antarctic Peninsula. I will write from there soon.

November 7

Dear Mom and Dad,

   Use after reading Chapter 19, Lesson 3, pages 662–667.

The Pacific Islands and Antarctica

Directions Complete this graphic organizer to show that you understand how to make predictions about the Pacific Islands and Antarctica.

WHAT YOU KNOW	+	WHAT YOU READ	=	PREDICTION	WHAT ACTUALLY HAPPENED

WHAT YOU KNOW +	WHAT YOU READ =	PREDICTION	WHAT ACTUALLY HAPPENED
Europeans changed life for people living in the Americas, Africa, South America, Asia, and Australia.	Pacific Islanders lived in isolation from the rest of the world until early European exploration expanded into the Pacific Ocean.	Students should indicate that Europeans will change the Pacific islanders' ways of life.	Students may list changes such as commercial farming, metal tools, new crops, Christianity, and western government.
The climate in Antarctica is very harsh and cold. This makes it difficult for plants to grow and people to live there. Seals, whales, penguins, and seabirds make Antarctica their home.	Antarctica is surrounded by the waters of the Atlantic, Pacific, and Indian Oceans. These waters support Antarctica's wildlife.	Possible answers include: Most of Antarctica's living resources are found in the waters surrounding it.	Students should mention that Antarctica's living resources include animal and plant life from the sea.

19 Test Preparation

Name _______________________ Date _______________

Directions Read each question and choose the best answer. Then fill in the circle for the answer you have chosen. Be sure to fill in the circle completely.

1 The island group that lies north of Australia and east of Indonesia is—
(A) Polynesia.
(B) Hawaii.
(C) New Zealand.
(D) Melanesia.

2 A _______ is a destructive tropical storm that occurs in the South Pacific.
(F) tsunami
(G) typhoon
(H) monsoon
(J) hurricane

3 Which island is a trust territory that is given protection and economic aid by the United States?
(A) New Guinea
(B) Tonga
(C) Solomon
(D) Guam

4 The icy continent of Antarctica has most of the world's supply of—
(F) moss.
(G) uranium.
(H) ice and fresh water.
(J) algae.

5 The emperor or the chinstrap is a species of _______ found in Antarctica.
(A) seal
(B) penguin
(C) whale
(D) albatross

Use after reading Chapter 19, pages 644–669.